Imagine a Woman
in Love with Herself

Imagine a Woman
in Love with Herself

EMBRACING YOUR WISDOM AND WHOLENESS

℘ ℘

Patricia Lynn Reilly

Preface by SARK
Foreword by Sue Patton Thoele

CONARI PRESS
Berkeley, California

Conari Press books are distributed by Publishers Group West.
Rose photographs (cover) by Deborah Schenk

Library of Congress Cataloging-in-Publication Data
Reilly, Patricia Lynn.
    Imagine a woman in love with herself : embracing your wisdom and wholeness / Patricia Lynn Reilly : preface by SARK : foreword by Sue Patton Theole.
        p.   cm.
    ISBN: 1-57324-169-5 (trade paper)
    1. Spiritual life. 2. Women—Religious life. I. Title.
B625.7.R47 1999
200'.82—dc21 99–16071
    CIP

Printed in the United States of America on recycled paper.
03 02 01 00 99 DATA 1 2 3 4 5 6 7 8 9 10

Preface

Dear Hearts...Conari Press and Patricia!

   Thank yu so kindly for asking me
to participate in this marvelous and
important book. I resonate so deeply
with all that is within its pages and
the reflection in my soul.

   Patricia, Bless yu and your work!!
Here are the words that came through

"Imagine a book created that
supports our actual and essence
selves. That's what this book is."

SARK
succulent wild woman

An Author, An Artist, A very Creative Company
WWW.CAMPSARK.COM

Foreword

Sue Patton Thoele
author of *The Courage to Be Yourself*

Patricia Lynn Reilly celebrates the wondrous and unique women we now are and the equally remarkable ones we are in the process of becoming. Falling head over heels in love with ourselves and learning to treat ourselves with the same respect, tender mercy, and gentle amusement we usually reserve for others actually facilitates our maturation into the women we were born to become.

However, acceptance and celebration of self is often hard to achieve, especially when we believe we've done or said something "wrong." Recently, for instance, I felt that I had made a fool of myself in the presence of my son's new girlfriend. The following morning, embarrassment and remorse threatened to lay a film of shame over my day and my self-esteem. Even my son's reassurance that my behavior was a "non-issue" failed to erase the self-blame in which I was indulging.

Thankfully, as time passed, I was able to view the incident less critically and with a welcome and healthy sense of humor. Maybe I could call myself the "Poster Girl for Imperfection" and, as Patricia encourages us to do, imagine myself as a woman who has access to a full range of human emotions and expresses them directly.

We need to honor every aspect of our personalities and spirits and recognize that the unusual and the imperfect parts are what make us rare, full, and radiant beings. To do so is an act of love and allegiance and, as captured in Patricia's writing, a powerful act of imagination: Imagine a woman who has grown in knowledge and love of herself. A woman who has vowed faithfulness to her own life and capacities. Who remains loyal to herself. Regardless.

From my own experience and from discussing the issue of self-love with countless other women, I've found that women have two essential tasks: 1) to embrace ourselves into wholeness—warts and wisdom alike—and 2) to believe in our own goodness, worth, and beauty. Because imagination leads to belief, *Imagine a Woman in Love with Herself* provides us with a clear and gentle path through the wilderness of self-doubt and deprecation into the joyous realm of unconditional love and belief in ourselves. Regardless. From such self-love flows a deeper and richer ability to love others and life itself.

Thank you, Patricia.

Your True Reflection

Imagine a Woman In Love With Herself is based on twenty stanzas of my popular poem, "Imagine a Woman." The book expresses the heart of my fifteen-year ministry supporting women to author their own lives, to name their own gods, and to grow in knowledge and love of themselves. Each chapter starts with a stanza of the poem and is followed by a series of woman-affirming reflections and meditations meant to carry you into your day . . . into your life.

In preparation for reading the book, read through the poem. As you do, imagine standing in front of a woman-affirming mirror. The book invites you to look upon yourself with loving-kindness. Gazing at your own *true* reflection, you will discover that everything you have longed for "out there" is already within you. It is my prayer that you will accept this book's invitation to descend into the richness of who you are, reclaim your inner resources, and grow in knowledge and love of yourself.

Our beloved planet is in desperate need of women who have moved from self-loathing to self-love, from self-criticism to self-celebration. Women who design woman-affirming solutions to the challenges confronting humankind as it enters the twenty-first century. Women who use their personal and communal resources to give birth to images of inclusion, poems of truth, rituals of healing, experiences of transformation, relationships of equality, and households of compassion. Women full of themselves!

Imagine a Woman

I

Imagine a woman who believes it is right and good she is woman.
A woman who honors her experience and tells her stories.
Who refuses to carry the sins of others within her body and life.

2

Imagine a woman who has acknowledged the past's influence
on the present.
A woman who has walked through her past.
Who has healed into the present.

3

Imagine a woman in love with her own body.
A woman who believes her body is enough, just as it is.
Who celebrates her body's rhythms and cycles as an exquisite resource.

4

Imagine a woman who embraces her sexuality as her own.
A woman who delights in pleasuring herself.
Who experiences her erotic sensations without shame or guilt.

5

Imagine a woman who honors the body of the Goddess in her
changing body.

A woman who celebrates the accumulation of her years and her wisdom.

Who refuses to use her precious life-energy disguising the changes in her
body and life.

6

~ 4

Imagine a woman who has access to the full range of human emotion.

A woman who expresses her feelings clearly and directly.

Who allows them to pass through her as gracefully as a breath.

7

Imagine a woman who tells the truth.

A woman who trusts her experience of the world and expresses it.

Who refuses to defer to the thoughts, perceptions, and responses of others.

8

Imagine a woman who follows her creative impulses.

A woman who produces original creations.

Who refuses to color inside someone else's lines.

9

Imagine a woman who names her own gods.
A woman who imagines the divine in her image and likeness.
Who designs a personal spirituality to inform her daily life.

10

Imagine a woman who refuses to surrender to gods, gurus, and higher powers.
A woman who has descended into her own inner life.
Who asserts her will in harmony with its impulses and instincts.

11

Imagine a woman who is interested in her own life.
A woman who embraces her life as teacher, healer, and challenge.
Who is grateful for the ordinary moments of beauty and grace.

12

Imagine a woman who authors her own life.
A woman who trusts her inner sense of what is right for her.
Who refuses to twist her life out of shape to meet the expectations of others.

13

Imagine a woman who participates in her own life.

A woman who meets each challenge with creativity.

Who takes action on her own behalf with clarity and strength.

14

Imagine a woman who has crafted a fully formed solitude.

A woman who is available to herself.

Who chooses friends and lovers with the capacity to respect her solitude.

15

Imagine a woman who refuses to diminish her life so others will feel better.

A woman who brings the fullness of her years, experience, and wisdom into each relationship.

Who expects others to be challenged and blessed by her presence in their lives.

16

Imagine a woman who assumes equality in her relationships.

A woman who no longer believes she is inferior to men and in need of their salvation.

Who has taken her rightful place beside them in the human community.

17

Imagine a woman who refuses to use her precious life-energy managing crisis and conflict.

A woman whose relationships deepen in satisfaction and contentment without depleting her.

Who chooses friends and lovers with the necessary skills to navigate through the challenges of life.

18

Imagine a woman who values the women in her life.

A woman who sits in circles of women.

Who is reminded of the truth about herself when she forgets.

19

Imagine a woman who has relinquished the desire for intellectual safety and approval.

A woman who makes a powerful statement with every word she speaks, every action she takes.

Who asserts to herself the right to reorder the world.

20

Imagine a woman who has grown in knowledge and love of herself.
A woman who has vowed faithfulness to her own life and capacities.
Who remains loyal to herself. Regardless.

Imagine yourself as this woman.

Imagine a Woman
in Love with Herself

I

Imagine a woman who believes it is right and good she is woman.

A woman who honors her experience and tells her stories.

Who refuses to carry the sins of others within her body and life.

In the Very Beginning
the Girl-Child Loves Herself

Our daughters, granddaughters, and nieces remind us that in the very beginning the girl-child loves herself. She comes into the world with feelings of omnipotence, not inferiority. She loves her body, expresses its needs, and follows its impulses. She recognizes and expresses her feelings. She tells the truth. She is interested in herself and enjoys private time. She is involved with herself and her own pursuits. She celebrates herself and expects acknowledgment for her creativity and accomplishments. She does not expend one ounce of her precious life-energy trying to figure out what is wrong with her body, feelings, and thoughts. She just lives. She makes a statement with every thought she shares, every feeling she expresses, and every action she takes on her own behalf.

Sadly, this season of the girl-child's life is short-lived. By the time she reaches junior high school, she has forgotten her original delight in herself. Her vision is narrowed; she sees the world as everyone else sees it. She loses her ability to act spontaneously; she acts as expected. Her original trust in herself is shattered; she waits to be told how to live. Her original spunk is exiled; she learns that it is dangerous to venture outside the lines. Her original goodness is twisted and labeled unnatural/unfeminine/too intense by the adults in her life. The girl-child emerges from adolescence with a poor self-image, relatively low expectations from life, and much less confidence in herself and her abilities than boys have in themselves.

She grows up asking, "What's wrong with me?" This question regularly punctuates women's lives from adolescence on as they search far and wide for someone to give them an answer, for someone to offer them a magical insight, treatment, or cure. Because we women have learned a criticism-based way of perceiving ourselves and relating to the world, our automatic tendency is to feel inadequate and that we're never quite good enough no matter what we do. The question "What's wrong with me?" does not develop within us naturally. On a personal level, the question is shaped over time by the critical words, images, experiences, and expectations of childhood. We become convinced something is wrong with us and that our life-task is to discover what it is.

A closer examination of the question, however, reveals the critical words, images, experiences, and expectations of many lifetimes of women convinced that something is wrong with them because of views expressed through theology, psychology, societal scripts, family customs, and intellectual and social history. Clearly, the question's presence within us is not an arbitrary occurrence. The belief that something is fundamentally, inherently wrong with women is woven into the fabric of Western civilization.

Many of us assume that our quest to discover what's wrong is particular and unique. Caught in the swirls of everyday living with its demands and challenges, we have no time to wonder about the larger dimensions of the question: Perhaps the very design of society itself does not sanction our full satisfaction and contentment. Perhaps it requires us to "fit in" at the expense of our sanity, health, and pride. Perhaps fitting in requires us to become alienated from ourselves, from all that is naturally and organically ours as Children of Life. Perhaps the question is much larger and more encompassing than we could ever have imagined: What's wrong with us? What's wrong with women? A mantra passed down from generation to generation . . . a mantra formulated by others.

There have always been women who remember the old ways.
Women who hold within them
the memory of a time
in the very beginning
when women were honored.

Women who refuse
to worship the gods,
to learn the language,
to take the names
of the fathers.

Women who refuse to twist
their female bodies out of shape
to fit into definitions,
to transcend limitations.
Women who love their bodies. Regardless.

Women who refuse to please others
by becoming smaller than they are.
Women who take up space
with their thoughts and feelings,
their needs and desires,
their anger and their dreams.

Women from every age
wild women
spinster women
wise women
rebellious women
women who love women
midwives
witches
healers
activists.

Banners and placards aloft . . .
Eve, the Mother of All Living
    Take and eat of the good fruit of life. Take a big bite!
Sappho
    She Who Gives Birth Has Power over Life and Death
Mary Wollstonecraft
    Break the Silken Fetters
Sojourner Truth
    Ain't I a Woman!

Margaret Sanger
Speak and Act in Defiance of Convention
Elizabeth Cady Stanton
Whatever the Bible may be made to do in Hebrew and Greek
in plain English it does not exalt and dignify women.
Karen Horney
Womb Envy Is More Like It
Audre Lorde
The Master's Tools Will Never Dismantle the Master's House

One by one the women step up
and speak the truth of a woman's life
they commit the forbidden act
of biting into patriarchal thought
refuting it, smashing it,
discarding it and beginning again
in the very beginning when women
loved their bodies
named their gods
authored their lives
when women refused to surrender
except to life as it pulsated through them.

Women full of themselves
their ideas
their stories
their anger
their passion.

Women reminding us
there is nothing wrong
there never has been anything wrong
there never will be anything wrong
with woman
that's why nothing ever works.
Stop asking the question!

One by one they step up and speak the truth
the truth of a woman's life
told with heart, mind, and body
refusing dissection
they are women and poets and theorists
who gather our brokenness
into their words
an impulse toward wholeness
awakens within us
and we become again
as we once were
whole.

Daughter of Woman, it is right and good that you are woman.
Honor your experience and tell your stories.
Refuse to carry the sins of others within your body and life.

The Mother of All Living

Imagine yourself as a leaf let go of by an autumn tree . . . a leaf slowly and gradually descending toward the ground . . . its descent cushioned by the breath of life . . . a leaf touching the ground in the forest deep within your being. You rise from the ground, thanking the leaf for transporting you so gently.

Everything breathes in the forest. Savor the breath of life flowing in and around you. Inhale deeply as the breath rises from the rich earth beneath you. Release the breath into the cool and moist air around you. Your attention moves upward and you notice the trees reaching arm in arm for the sky. You become a tree. Your feet grow roots extending deep into the ground. Your arms become branches stretching high into the sky. You sway with the breeze. The birds of the forest dance with you as they leap from branch to branch. You see many things from your new height.

A nearby stream calls to you, "Come and play." In a moment, you are at the stream, splashing in its bouncing waters. As you are drying off in the warm sunlight pouring through the forest canopy, a path opens up before you and invites you to follow it to a special place. You accept the invitation. The path leads you deep within the forest to the edge of a clearing . . . a magical open space surrounded by a ring of ancient redwoods, forming an outer circle, and by a sparkling stream, forming an inner circle. You cross the stream. You enter the clearing.

A woman approaches you: "The Mother of All Living is waiting. She has a story to tell you. Come, let us meet her in the center of the clearing." You see the Mother at a distance. You approach her with your arms at your sides. You feel no shame in her presence. Her eyes meet yours and in her gaze you are recognized . . . shaken . . . and relieved. She embraces you and you become as you once were . . . fully present and in love with yourself. She tells you stories of a time that once was . . .

Of ancient beliefs in a Great Mother who gave birth to the cosmos and its inhabitants, both human and divine; of ancient times when it was from the mother, the giver of life, that the line of the generations was traced; of ancient women who did not apologize for their fertile wombs, pregnant bellies, and full breasts; women who celebrated themselves as the embodiment of the Great Mother and who celebrated the birth of their daughters.

Of ancient beliefs that celebrated the Great Mother's "moon blood," spilling from her to create all that is. Of ancient ways that held a woman's blood to be magic, flowing in harmony with the moon. Of ancient times when the color of royalty was the dark red wine color of woman's beautiful blood. Of ancient women who did not apologize for their bodies or for their bleeding time.

Of ancient times when women were honored for their capacities both to nurture and to accomplish great things, when virginity meant "woman, complete in herself, owned by no man, creator of her own destiny." Of ancient women who did not apologize for their power, courage, and independence, who refused to surrender except to their truest self and wisest voice.

Of ancient beliefs in the Crone Goddess, representing old age, winter, and the waning of the moon. Of ancient societies that celebrated the accumulation of a woman's years and respected the menopausal retaining of her wise blood. Of ancient post-menopausal women who presided at sacred rituals and ceremonies, who did not apologize for the fullness of their years and their wisdom.

Women from every age join you in the clearing. Their song calls to you: "You who stand apart, come close. You who are out of touch, come near." They do not throw stones, instead they give you flowers and embrace you with joy. They sing to you: "It is right and good that you are woman."

Breathing in . . . I honor my experience.
    Breathing out . . . And tell my stories.
Breathing in . . . I refuse to carry the sins of others
    Breathing out . . . Within my body and life.
Breathing in . . . I turn toward myself with dignity.
    Breathing out . . . It is right and good that I am woman.

The Maternal Deep

Sit in front of a large bowl of water. In the Middle Ages, wells were a sacred symbol for the pagan community. They were considered passageways to the underground womb, the maternal deep. Pagans visited the wells and prayed to the resident goddess, asking her to meet their heart's desire. Because wells celebrated the feminine principle, clergymen denounced them as "devilish cunts," believing that female devil-nymphs lived in them. They eventually outlawed all well ceremonies.

Imagine that the bowl in front of you is a well filled with living water. Reach into it and play with the water while breathing deeply.

Breathing in . . . Water
Breathing out . . . Moistening, flowing, yielding, cleansing.
Breathing in . . . Water
Breathing out . . . Soothing, cooling, healing, refreshing.
Breathing in . . . Water
Breathing out . . . The cosmic womb, the maternal deep.
Breathing in . . . Water
Breathing out . . . The menstrual flow from Mother Earth.

Gaze deeply into the well and discover yourself. You are the holy nymph, the well's resident deity. Take healing water from the well and bless your body with it.

Breathing in . . . I turn toward my body with loving-kindness.
    Breathing out . . . Blessed is my body.

Gaze deeply into the well and discover yourself. You are the holy nymph, the resident deity of the well. Take soothing water from the well and splash yourself with it.

Breathing in . . . I turn toward myself with joy.
    Breathing out . . . It is right and good that I am woman.

2

Imagine a woman who has acknowledged the past's influence on the present.

A woman who has walked through her past.

Who has healed into the present.

Healing into the Present

There were times when my childhood imagination soared as I imagined another childhood—one with loving parents. While in St. Joseph's Village, an institution for dependent children, I became a popular tour guide on Saturday and Sunday afternoons. Kindhearted Catholic families from northern New Jersey stopped by to tour the spacious complex and to meet the "orphans." Besides making lots of money, prompting the nuns to instate a restriction on the amount I could keep, I was examining each family for new qualities to add to my "loving family" fantasy. I watched the way the parents looked at their children: Were their eyes filled with gentleness or harshness? I listened to the tone of voice they used in conversation with their children: Were their voices patient or irritable? I paid special attention to how they touched their children: Were the exchanges affectionate or rough? By the end of an afternoon, I knew who the kindest families were and hoped they would ask for permission to take me home for a weekend . . . or a lifetime. And most of them did ask. I spent many weekends with kind families who nourished my imaginative fantasies of the family I wanted—one that kept its children. Throughout my life, I have adopted families, chosen-families, who have looked at me with gentleness, who have spoken to me with respect, and who have touched me with affection. One by one, I have "imagined into being" the powerful visions I developed in reaction and response to childhood realities.

My childhood fantasizing was not a unique experience. Women write detailed accounts of their comforting childhood fantasies. Some women imagined into being whole new worlds inhabited by families who loved, respected, and protected their children. Other women, discontent with only a few aspects of their family life, imagined into being "rehabilitated" family members. In the solitude of their imaginations, whether creating new families or rehabilitating the familiar cast of characters, they developed intricate dialogues and interactions between family members.

Their dialogues reflect three longings that appear repeatedly in women's writings: the longing to be acknowledged, listened to, and taken seriously; the longing to be free of household responsibility; and the longing for their parents to love each other. For some, their flights of fancy were inspired and nourished by the unconditional love of a grandmother or by nonargumentative dinners at a best friend's house. Each child-friendly fantasy and experience settled into our being as a seed of promise, reminding us that things could be different and that our fantasies were not vain imaginings. In the fullness of time, the seeds of promise bear fruit in a healthy life in the present.

To heal into the present, we must enlist the transformational capacities of our imaginations. Based on this conviction, I have developed a series of "Healing into the Present Meditations" and "Healthy Family Fantasies." Throughout *Imagine a Woman in Love with Herself,* you will be invited to enter into these meditations and fantasies. They will reawaken and inspire your imagination, support your healing into the present, and challenge you to design a woman-affirming life and home.

Daughter of Woman, acknowledge the past's influence on the present.
Walk through your past.
Heal into the present.

A New Birth

Imagine yourself as a leaf let go of by an autumn tree . . . a leaf slowly and gradually descending toward the ground . . . its descent cushioned by the breath of life . . . a leaf touching the ground in the forest deep within your being. You rise from the ground, thanking the leaf for transporting you so gently.

Everything breathes in the forest. Savor the breath of life flowing in and around you. Inhale deeply as the breath rises from the rich earth beneath you. Release the breath into the cool and moist air around you. Your attention moves upward and you notice the trees reaching arm in arm for the sky. You become a tree. Your feet grow roots extending deep into the ground. Your arms become branches stretching high into the sky. You sway with the breeze. The birds of the forest dance with you as they leap from branch to branch. You see many things from your new height.

A nearby stream calls to you, "Come and play." In a moment, you are at the stream, splashing in its bouncing waters. As you are drying off in the warm sunlight pouring through the forest canopy, a path opens up before you and invites you to follow it to a special place. You accept the invitation. The path leads you deep within the forest to the edge of a clearing . . . a magical open space surrounded by a ring of ancient redwoods, forming the outer circle, and by a sparkling stream, forming the inner circle. You cross the stream. You enter the clearing.

A woman approaches you: "The Mother of All Living is waiting. She has a story to tell you. Come, let us meet her in the center of the clearing." You see the Mother at a distance. You approach her with your arms at your sides. You feel no shame in her presence. Her eyes meet yours and in her gaze you are recognized . . . shaken . . . and relieved. She embraces you and you become as you once were . . . fully present and in love with yourself. She tells you the story of the Divine Girl-Child whose birth was announced and celebrated by angels, whose coming merited visitors and precious gifts, and in whose honor the peoples of the world gather for a yearly retelling of the story of her birth.

In this hour everything is stillness. There is total silence and awe.
We are overwhelmed with a great wonder. We keep vigil.
We are expecting the coming of the Divine Girl-Child.

In the fullness of time, she is born.
She shines like the sun, bright and beautiful.
She is laughing a most joyful laugh.
She is a delight, soothing the world with peace.

Become bold. Lean over and look at her.
Touch her face. Lift her in your hands with great awe.
Look at her more closely. There is no blemish on her.
She is splendid to see.

She opens her eyes and looks intently at you.
A powerful light comes forth from her eyes, like a flash of
    lightning.
The light of her gaze invites the hidden one to come into the
    light.
The sleeping one to awaken. The frozen one to thaw.
The buried one to emerge. The hard and protected one to soften.
Receive her healing gaze deep within your being.

Suddenly there appears a multitude of heavenly beings singing:
"Glory to the Mother of All Living and to her Daughter.
She has arrived. The Divine Child is among us.
She will bring peace and inspire goodwill among all people.

Welcome her joyfully. Shout with a loud voice:
You belong here among us. We're glad you're alive!

Surround her with goodness, safety, and laughter.
She is the Divine Child, come among us this day.
Celebrate the Girl-Child, born in all ages.
Come to bring us salvation and grace."

Breathing in . . . I look upon myself with loving-kindness.
Breathing out . . . There is no blemish.
Breathing in . . . I celebrate my birth.
Breathing out . . . It is right and good that I'm alive.

Sorrow and Joy

Walk through the years of your life, beginning with your birth. Count the years in your mind's eye: one, two, three, four. . . . Pay special attention to the years that hurt as you pass through them. Call aloud the number of each hurtful year. Bless the bruised and wounded years.

Breathing in . . . As deep a cavern as sorrow has carved within me,
Breathing out . . . That shall be my capacity for joy.
Breathing in . . . I bless the bruised and wounded years.
Breathing out . . . There is no blemish.

Now travel again through the years, beginning with your birth. Count the years in your mind's eye: one, two, three, four. . . . This time pay special attention to the years that delight you as you pass through them. Call aloud the number of each delightful year. Celebrate the bright and comfortable years.

Breathing in . . . I turn toward my life with loving-kindness.
  Breathing out . . . Blessed be my years.
Breathing in . . . I celebrate the bright and comfortable years.
  Breathing out . . . There is no blemish.

Gather all the years of your life, the bright and the bruised. Call out the accumulation of your years.

Breathing in . . . I have acknowledged the past's influence on the present.
  Breathing out . . . I have walked through my past.
Breathing in . . . I have healed into the present.
  Breathing out . . . Blessed be my life.

3

Imagine a woman in love with her own body.

A woman who believes her body is enough, just as it is.

Who celebrates her body's rhythms and cycles as an exquisite resource.

The Exuberance
of the Universe

In the very beginning, the girl-child's body is full of energy, movement, and sound. She lives a body-centered existence and is naturally exuberant. She releases her big bundle of body-energy through movements and sounds. She runs and jumps, climbs and explores, throws and hits. She cries, moans, and screams. She shouts, sings, and hums. And even her occasional "tantrum" at the end of a long day serves to release her pent-up energy before sleep. Every body-movement and expression teaches her where she ends and others begin. Early on she doesn't know the difference between hitting a chair and hitting her brother, between climbing on the couch and climbing on Grandma's precious antique chair. Her senses are alive and attuned to the world around her. She is naturally curious about the sight, sound, taste, feel, and smell of things. Most of what she will learn in the first five years of life, she will learn through her body and its capacities. It is her teacher, healer, and challenge. No separation exists between her mind and her body. They are one within her. The exuberance of the universe pulsates through her. She loves herself.

As we grew, our natural exuberance and body-centeredness were criticized as unladylike (not feminine enough) or tomboyish (too masculine) by our families. We were offered fewer opportunities than our brothers to develop our physical capacities and to stretch our bodies to their physical limits. Our brothers were taught to throw a ball. They were encouraged to play baseball. A girl's place was in the home not on the field, we were told. We were expected to wear shoes and clothes that made it impossible for us to run, jump, and keep up with the boys. We were expected to limit the space we took up with our voices. A certain tone of voice was encouraged—wimpy and passive sounds that reflected our restraint. We were expected to limit the space we took up with our bodies: "ladies" sat still with their legs together or crossed. We were required to conform to these childhood commandments at the expense of our exuberance and healthy body-centeredness.

Some of us conformed and became quintessential females to win the approval of our parents and to survive childhood. Sufficiently restrained, our natural body-energy was directed away from body-activity toward body-grooming, away from spontaneity toward control. Groomed to be "ornamental," we spent inordinate amounts of time and resources twisting our bodies into the acceptable shapes of the culture. Some of us rebelled and refused to twist our bodies out of shape. We identified with the boys and sought to transcend the "weakness" of being female. We assumed an androgynous demeanor and attitude. Thus we were unacceptable to the "ornamental" girls but we never quite fit in among the boys either. Whatever our choice, we became convinced something was wrong with our body and its natural impulses toward activity and exuberance. Those of us who chose ornamentalism denied these impulses as "unfeminine." Those of us who chose a male-defined androgyny embraced them as "boyish." Either way, the girl-child's original goodness was twisted out of shape and labeled unacceptable by her family and, eventually, by herself.

Reminded of the truth about ourselves, we reclaim our woman-bodies. Consciousness of the breath escorts us home to our bodies. In the very beginning of our lives, we breathed deeply into the belly. A healthy breath begins in the abdomen and moves upward toward the chest and then is released downward toward the belly. Each time we were criticized in our childhood homes, this deep belly breath was reversed and we developed the habit of shallow breathing into the upper chest while chronically tightening our abdominal muscles. We inherited this "fight or flight" survival breath from our earliest ancestors. Our socialization sets us up either to "fight" against the natural self by banishing it to a subterranean basement of our being, holding it back lest an unscrutinized need, uncensored feeling, or spontaneous thought slip out—or to take "flight" from the natural self by participating in countless distractions. A shallow breath is evidence of our alienation from the deepest parts of ourselves.

As we return home to the deep breath we knew in the very beginning, our original body-centeredness is reestablished. With each breath, we actively nourish the body, balance its systems, listen to the wisdom of its sensations, and participate fully in every body-centered activity. Consider the following benefits of deep breathing:

- Conscious breathing treats the body to a feast of nourishment. A deep inhalation nourishes a larger quantity of blood cells than a shallow breath. A full exhalation releases the accumulation of carbon monoxide. A shallow breath leaves residues of this waste product within our systems and supplies our bodies with only enough nourishment to function at a minimal level.

- Conscious breathing balances all of the systems of the body. It lowers the blood pressure, massages the internal organs, supports the digestive processes, and aids in the body's eliminatory functions. A shallow breath is only capable of supporting the body's processes on a superficial level.

- Conscious breathing supports us to pause in the midst of our busy lives to pay attention to our bodily sensations. They are the voice of our organic needs for food, rest, orgasm, exercise, elimination, and touch. With each deep breath, we become more skillful at discerning the intention and wisdom of each sensation. And as we step into self-responsibility, we meet the needs of our bodies with tenderness and grace.

- Conscious breathing is our opportunity to participate with the body in each of its adventures. As we become more attuned to the flow of the breath, we develop our capacity to direct it into any part of the body to enhance sexual sensations or to relieve painful ones. We learn to savor every sensation as it rises, and then to let it go with a blessing as it passes. To breathe deeply is to participate fully in all aspects of our lives.

Initially women are uncomfortable turning toward their bodies with tenderness and conscious, prolonged attention. Their discomfort makes great sense. Our bodies have borne the brunt of our self-criticism. Most women scrutinize every detail of their bodies under an unmerciful magnifying glass. They inspect their bodies, searching for flaws: too big, too small; too much, too little; too round, too flat; too tall, too short. Over time, we develop a chronic resentment toward our bodies because they are always falling short of perfection as defined by the culture, our families, a current lover, and ourselves. They are never quite good enough no matter what we do to them. Notice your own discomfort without judgment, and then imagine the discomfort riding on the back of the breath, to be released with each exhalation.

As we turn a merciful eye toward our bodies, we reverse our harsh scrutiny and chronic resentment of them. We come home to our bodies as they are and commit the forbidden act, the essential political act, of loving our bodies as we did in the very beginning of our lives. A woman who loves herself honors her body as the sacred temple of the spirit of life. She embraces it as a community of support within her, a harmonious partnership of cells, tissues, organs, and systems. She enters into a partnership with her body, improving conscious contact with it through meditation, and consulting it through each season of her life. She pays attention to its sensations as faithful reminders of the way home. She celebrates her body as an exquisite resource, a faithful ally, and a trustworthy companion.

Daughter of Woman, love your body.
It is enough, just as it is.
Celebrate its rhythms and cycles as an exquisite resource.

Come Home to Your Breath

Come home to your breath. Turn your attention inward by taking two deep breaths. Become conscious of the breath and its faithful rhythm, supporting you through the length of your days. Savor the breath of life as it flows in, through, and around you.

As you inhale, gather all of yourself from the far reaches of your life. As you exhale, allow sighs, sounds, and yawns to ride on the back of your breath, releasing the accumulation of your day. Weave an affirmation into each breath:

Breathing in . . . I come home to my breath.
    Breathing out . . . Home is always waiting.

Breathing in . . . I gather my attention home.
    Breathing out . . . I release the demands of the day.
Breathing in . . . I gather my attention home.
    Breathing out . . . I release the challenges of the day.
Breathing in . . . I gather my attention home.
    Breathing out . . . I release the interactions of the day.

Breathing in . . . I come home to my breath.
Breathing out . . . Home is always waiting.

Notice the depth of your breath.

- ↬ Place your hands on your upper chest. Inhale, expanding your chest with the breath. Exhale. This is a shallow breath. Breathe into your upper chest for two more breaths.

- ↬ Now place your hands on the sides of your rib cage—the middle chest. Inhale deeply, pushing the breath against your ribs. Exhale. Continue to fill your rib cavity for two more breaths, deepening your capacity to hold the nourishing breath of life.

- ↬ Now place your hands on your abdomen. Inhale deeply into the abdomen, imagining the breath as a great wave filling your belly. Allow your belly to swell. This is a deep breath. Exhale as the wave retreats, leaving nourishment in its wake. Continue to breathe deeply into your belly for two more breaths.

- ↬ Now place your hands on your lower back. Breathe into your lower back, the location of your kidneys, the well of life-giving energy within you. Allow this deep breath to nourish you, to enrich you, to fill you. Continue to breathe deeply into your lower back for two more breaths.

- ↬ Bring your arms to your sides and continue to breathe deeply. Inhale, as the full swell moves upward from your abdomen, into your rib cavity, and then into the upper chest. Exhale, as the wave retreats downward from your chest, your rib cavity, and your abdomen, leaving serenity in its wake. Continue this deep breathing for two more breaths.

Breathing in . . . I come home to my breath.
Breathing out . . . Home is always waiting.

You Are Enough

Imagine standing in your favorite place in the natural world. Allow your bare feet to touch the earth. Feel the firm ground supporting you. A circle of benches appears. Sit in the middle of the circle. You are waiting for a beloved grandmother, mentor, teacher, friend, or mythic image to arrive.

In the fullness of time, she walks into the circle and sits across from you. She will lead you in a meditation of acknowledgment. She invites you to bless your woman-body by moving or stretching it, touching or massaging it, or directing the breath into each part of your body in response to her suggestions. Imagine her saying:

"You are enough. You are blessed. Hold nothing in.
Allow your body to take its shape. Love the shape of your body."

Begin at the top of your head.
  Acknowledge your head. Move it. Massage it.
Love your hair. Touch it now. Stroke it. Twirl it.
  Bless its curls, its straightness, its color, its texture.
Love your eyes. Bless their color. Massage your eyelids and eyebrows.
  Open and close them. Honor your unique view of the world.
Love your ears. Bless their shape and size. Massage them.
  Love your unique reception of the world.
Love your nose. Bless its shape and size.

  Breathe in and out slowly.
  Honor the Breath of Life as it passes through you.
Love your mouth and lips. Trace the shape of your lips.
  Love the sounds of your mouth. Make a sound.
Love your neck. Stroke it.
  Hold it up high. Massage it tenderly.
Love your shoulders. Raise them to your ears.
  Listen to them. Is there tension?
  Release them, and all they carry, with love.
Love your arms. Raise them up in front of you.
  Pat your hands together. Shake them. Kiss them.
Love your breasts. Firm, sagging, full, flat, beautiful as they are.
  Trace the shape of your breasts.
Love your abdomen. Fill it with your breath.
  Honor its roundness. Allow it to take its shape.
Trace the shape of your bottom. Honor the shape of your bottom.
  Massage it tenderly in appreciation for its faithful support.

At your own pace, slowly move, touch, or imagine each of the remaining parts of your body: your thighs, knees, calves, feet, and toes. Bless your woman-body by personalizing the following affirmation:

Breathing in . . . My thighs are good just as they are.
    Breathing out . . . There is no blemish.
Breathing in . . . My knees are good just as they are.
    Breathing out . . . There is no blemish.
Breathing in . . . My calves are good just as they are.
    Breathing out . . . There is no blemish.
Breathing in . . . My feet are good just as they are.
    Breathing out . . . There is no blemish.

To conclude, weave an affirmation into the breath:
Breathing in . . . My body is enough.
    Breathing out . . . Just as it is.
Breathing in . . . My body is good.
    Breathing out . . . There is no blemish.

4

Imagine a woman who embraces her sexuality as her own.

A woman who delights in pleasuring herself.

Who experiences her erotic sensations without shame or guilt.

The Sensuality
of the Universe

In the very beginning of her life, the girl-child is acquainted with the erotic energy within her. Childhood is not a time of sexual dormancy for the girl-child. From birth, she is capable of sexual arousal and orgasm. These are her birthrights as a child of life. She says a big "YES" to life as it pulsates through her. She feels the "YES" in her curiosity about her body's sensations and in her exploration of its fascinating nooks and crannies, openings and operations. Her body is her closest friend. She discovers her clitoris and receives pleasure from touching it. She experiences her body's sensuality by feeling its smoothness and curves, by touching its lips, by entering its openings, by tasting its juiciness, and by delighting in its natural fragrances. She also feels the "YES" in her heart, her joy, and even in her tears. It touches every area of her life. The erotic potential of the universe pulsates through her. She loves herself.

Eventually, our original erotic potential was judged as unfeminine, immodest, and impure by our parents' words and actions. For those of us who were touched affectionately by our parents, touch was seldom extended beyond early childhood. As we matured and grew out of the "cute stage," our parents became uncomfortable with our developing bodies and most touching abruptly stopped. We created stories to make sense of this withdrawal of affection. We became convinced something was wrong with our bodies—that our growing breasts, pubic hair, and the genital sensations we were experiencing made us untouchable to our parents. For some of us, the incestuous behavior of a parent or relative compounded this growing discomfort.

In adolescence, the vagina replaces the clitoris as the focus of sexual pleasure in a culture that reduces sexuality to genital intercourse defined by the needs and desires of men. We accepted a form of sexuality that required a partner and that did not guarantee our satisfaction. And because our early body-knowing and erotic autonomy were not cultivated by our parents, we eventually became ignorant of the mechanics of female sexuality and dependent on others to meet our needs. We forgot about the wonders of our own bodies, their rich erotic potential, and their capacity for sensual delight and satisfaction. Our original love of our body, our curiosity about its sensations, and our exploration of its fascinating nooks and crannies were twisted out of shape and labeled unacceptable by our families and by ourselves.

Reminded of the truth about ourselves, we come home to our own sexuality. We rediscover the wonders of our own bodies, their rich erotic potential, and their capacity for sensual delight. We take responsibility for our own sexual pleasure and satisfaction, developing self-pleasuring rituals that continue even while we are in a sexual relationship. Through these rituals, we grow more in love with our bodies, we discover what arouses us, we develop an understanding of our sexual wounds and armoring, and we deepen in satisfaction and contentment with ourselves. We have come to believe that a personal sex life is an essential prerequisite to sharing healthy sexual intimacy with a partner.

Imagine hearing words of healing and affirmation read from a special book entitled "The Book of Woman" in your childhood church or home. Imagine hearing them today as She Who is Complete in Herself reminds you of what you knew in the very beginning of your life. She calls you home to your body, to your natural instincts, and to your sexual desires. She will inspire your erotic energy and imagination. Enter into her words.

I am Woman. I stride the earth in nakedness.
No robes hide the beauty of my fertile womb,
    my rounded belly, and my full breasts.
I am She Who is Complete in Herself.
I live in my body. I embrace its desires as my own.

Daughter of Woman,
The Goddesses loved themselves to their edges.
Self-possessed, they strode the Earth.
Embracing their sexuality as their own.
Delighting in pleasuring themselves.
Experiencing their erotic sensations without shame.

Daughter of Woman, own yourself completely.
Embark on an intimate journey into yourself.
Connect with the whole and complete center within you.
Experience fullness, self-possession, and satisfaction.

Delight in your freedom to be alone.
To meet your own needs. To give yourself pleasure.

Daughter of Woman, your body is your own. It is no one else's.
Live in your body. Trust its natural instincts.
Experience the pleasure of your body's sensuality.
Feel its smoothness and its curves.
Touch its lips. Enter its openings.
Taste its juiciness. Delight in its natural fragrances.
Explore the edges of your sensuality.

Daughter of Woman, feel the fire awaken within you.
Fire rising from the depths. Lover uncoiling to meet lover.
Height calling to depth. Earth moving toward heaven.
Celebrate the sensations in your genitals.
They are calling you to your edges.

Daughter of Woman, all the feelings in your body are good.
The tingling. The pulsations of pleasure.
The swelling to overflowing.
Honor all that has been demeaned.
Receive all that has been cast aside.
Your sexuality is good. It is very good.

.   *Daughter of Woman, embrace your sexuality.*
Delight in pleasuring yourself.
Experience all of your erotic sensations without shame or guilt.

The Source of Life

According to Eastern teachings, the body contains seven energy centers called chakras. The second chakra is located between the pubis and navel. It is connected to our capacity to create and to be sexual. There is an acupressure point located three finger-widths below the belly button. The Chinese call it the "Sea of Energy." Place your hands on your belly with the tips of your index fingers meeting in the center at the "Sea of Energy" point. This powerful acupressure point strengthens the reproductive system and supports self-confidence.

Begin and end the day with the "Source of Life" meditation. As you become familiar with the movements, create your own meditation.

Sitting, with both hands on your belly,
Breathing in . . . Source of Life,
  Breathing out . . . To you I come.
Breathing in . . . Welcoming is your womb,
  Breathing out . . . Nurturing is your love.
Breathing in . . . In you,
  Breathing out . . . I am enclosed and sustained.

Standing with your legs apart and your knees slightly bent.
Breathe in with both hands on your belly . . . *Source of Life,*
  Breathe out as your hands move downward
    from your belly through to the space

between your legs and then out
in front of you . . . *From you I am pushed.*

Breathe in, bringing hands to belly . . . *Strong is your womb,*
    Breathe out as your hands move downward
        from your belly through to the space
        between your legs and then out
        in front of you . . . *Powerful its thrust.*

Breathe in, bringing hands to belly . . . *In you,*
    Breathe out as your hands move downward
        from your belly through to the space
        between your legs and then out
        in front of you . . . *I exert, initiate, and move.*

To conclude the meditation, bring your hands to your belly, fingertips
meeting in the center. Weave an affirmation into the breath:
Breathing in . . . In gratitude,
    Breathing out . . . I acknowledge the Source of Life.

There Is No Blemish

Create a sacred space within your bathroom. In this space, your body
is cared for intimately. Surround your tub with flowers and candles.
Fill the space with woman-affirming music and images.

Buy a blanket-sized towel to hold you after the bath. Tape the blessing in your own voice. Include your favorite meditation music in the background. Draw your bath. Light the candles.

Imagine the tub as a well filled with living water. Reach into it and play with the water as you weave the following invocation into each breath:

Breathing in . . . Water
   Breathing out . . . Moistening, flowing, yielding, cleansing.
Breathing in . . . Water
   Breathing out . . . Soothing, cooling, healing, refreshing.
Breathing in . . . Water
   Breathing out . . . The cosmic womb, the maternal deep.
Breathing in . . . Water
   Breathing out . . . The menstrual flow from mother earth.
Breathing in . . . Water
   Breathing out . . . The impulse of creation, the beginning of all things.

With great compassion, bless yourself with healing water. Take the soothing, healing water from your bath, and bless your body with it, saying: *"Blessed am I. My body is good. It is very good. There is no blemish."*

With great compassion, bless the parts of your body it has been most difficult to acknowledge. Pay special attention to these areas—a scar, a place trespassed by another, a layer of protective fat, an untouchable part. Breathe into any discomfort without judgment. Notice what is true for you without shame. Affirm: *"My breasts (belly, clitoris, vagina . . .) are good. They are for my pleasure and delight. I am not ashamed of them. They are blessed."*

With great tenderness, sing or speak these words to yourself:
"The world within me is restored in beauty.
The world around me is restored in beauty.
The world behind me is restored in beauty.
The world before me is restored in beauty.
The world above me is restored in beauty.
The world below me is restored in beauty.
My body is restored in beauty."

5

Imagine a woman who honors the body of the Goddess in her changing body.

A woman who celebrates the accumulation of her years and her wisdom.

Who refuses to use her precious life-energy disguising the changes in her body and life.

The Circle
of Life

The Old Woman is the culmination of everything she has experienced since childhood. All along, the natural occurrences of our lives have been unacceptable: our "girlness," our bleeding, and our changing bodies during puberty and pregnancy. It makes great sense that we would continue the battle with our woman-bodies into a new frontier, the aging process. As our bodies change, we twist them out of shape in order to live up to society's expectation that a woman should never grow old.

Sadly, our self-hatred has reached such depths by this time that many women will do anything to get rid of the evidence of their aging. Some become obsessed and keep track of their wrinkles with a magnifying glass. Others submit to regular and painful injections of collagen. Still others resort to cosmetic surgery—the knife cutting away unwanted pieces of themselves, a bit of nose here, a piece of thigh there, a double chin, an unwanted bulge, wrinkle, or spot. Few celebrate their changing face and body. We can't imagine a god who wrinkles as we do.

Disguising the signs of aging consumes a great deal of a woman's energy. Little is left to deal with the economic and social factors that threaten her survival in a world that prefers men. Often her money has been spent on clothes, diets, and dyes instead of being set aside for the future. Her focus has been riveted on getting and keeping a man, who will then be her salvation, security, and companion into old age. The overwhelming reality, however, is that most women grow old alone, outliving all of their "saviors," and outlasting their saviors' bank accounts.

Reminded of a time when god looked like us, we discover that we are surrounded by a courageous company of women. Their ancient stories and images become healing resources for us. We learn of ancient women who did not apologize for their later years. We recall ancient societies that celebrated the accumulation of a woman's years and respected the menopausal retaining of a woman's wise blood. We read of ancient ways in which only post-menopausal women could preside at rituals and sacred rites. We learn of ancient beliefs in the Triple Goddess—Maiden, Mother, and Crone.

Just as the changing face of the Moon transforms the night sky, so the changing face of god transforms our images of aging and death. The Goddess who looks like us changes as we do. In the fullness of time, she becomes the Crone Goddess who wisely brings an allotted life-span to its end. She represents old age, winter, and the waning moon. She holds life and death as one within her. Neither is elevated or despised in the endless cycle of birth, life, death, and rebirth.

Inspired by Her, ancient women didn't view death as a passage to heaven but as a return to the Earth. These women weren't obsessed with aging and death. The old ones among them were considered as awesome as the Earth's sacred sites. They were revered because they held the wisdom of the Earth within their cracks, crevices, lines, and years. Each woman honored the body of the Goddess in her own changing body.

Inspired by images of the Goddess, we are healing the shame that accompanies our bodies, our natural processes, and our aging. We refuse to spend our precious life-energy hiding our bodies, disguising the signs of aging, and keeping the realities of our lives a secret. Rather, we celebrate the accumulation of our years and wisdom and the changes in our bodies and lives. We choose relationships with women and men who have the depth and the courage to embrace all of who we are now and will become in the next decades of our lives. We choose partners who have acknowledged their own issues around women's bodies, natural processes, and aging. Partners who are not interested in women as ornaments. Partners who attract powerful women as partners, friends, and lovers.

Daughter of Woman, honor the body of the Goddess in your changing body.
Celebrate the accumulation of your years and wisdom.
Refuse to use your precious life-energy disguising the changes in your body and life.

Gathering the Years

Move forward through the years, beginning with your birth. Pay special attention to the difficult years as you pass through them. If you are moved, draw the hurtful experiences, write about the painful exchanges, or dance the awkward moments. When your are finished, bless them by adding a healing color to your drawing, symbol to your writing, or movement to your dance.

Breathing in . . . In gratitude, I gather my years.
　　Breathing out . . . There is no blemish.
Breathing in . . . I bless the difficult years and hurtful experiences,
　　Breathing out . . . The painful exchanges and awkward moments.
Breathing in . . . In gratitude, I gather my years.
　　Breathing out . . . There is no blemish.

↝ 57

Travel again through the years of your life. This time, pay special attention to the delightful years as you pass through them. If you are moved, draw the joyful experiences, write about the comfortable exchanges, or dance the bright moments. When you are finished, celebrate them by adding a celebratory color to your drawing, symbol to your writing, or movement to your dance.

Breathing in . . . In gratitude, I gather my years
　　Breathing out . . . There is no blemish.
Breathing in . . . I celebrate the delightful years and joyful experiences.

Breathing out . . . The comfortable exchanges and bright moments.
Breathing in . . . In gratitude, I gather the years.
Breathing out . . . There is no blemish.

Gather all of the years of your life, the delightful and the difficult, on an altar of remembrance. Display the drawings, read your writings, enter into your dance of remembrance. Call out your age. Fill the space with the accumulation of your years. When finished, sit quietly at the altar. Breathe into the fullness of your years.

Breathing in . . . In gratitude, I gather the accumulation of my years.
Breathing out . . . There is no blemish.
Breathing in . . . The delightful and the difficult.
Breathing out . . . I acknowledge them all with gratitude.

Bless Your Changing Body

Turn your attention inward by taking two deep breaths. Imagine standing in a clearing deep within the forest of your being. You are surrounded by ancient redwoods. Take two more deep breaths.

Breathing in . . . The breath rises up from the rich earth beneath me.
Breathing out . . . I release the breath into the cool moist air around me.
Breathing in . . . I savor the breath of life
Breathing out . . . As it flows in and through and around me.

The Wise Old Woman invites you to sit beside the stream of living water, surrounding the clearing. Hear Her words: "Reach into the stream. Bless your changing body with its healing waters. Take a gentle walk over and around your body. Acknowledge the changes with tenderness. I am emerging within you. There is nothing to fear."

At your own pace, acknowledge your changing body. Beginning at your feet and slowly moving to your head, acknowledge each change: the lines, wrinkles, spots; the loosening, lowering, and stretching; the changes in color, shape, and texture. As you bless your changing body with the stream's holy water, create an affirmation for each change:

"My feet have carried me for _____ years. They hold the memory of each step I have taken to be here, now."

"My textured legs and pumping veins have supported my weight and the weight of _____ children."

"My bottom is looser now. I have let go. I am not as tight and guarded."

"My belly is rounded now. The challenges of life have stretched me beyond the limitations of youth."

"My muscles are wiser now. They tell me to go more slowly and thoughtfully through life."

"My shoulders signal when I need to meditate and release tension."

Conclude your meditation by weaving an affirmation into each breath.

Breathing in . . . I honor the body of the goddess
    Breathing out . . . In my changing body.
Breathing in . . . I refuse to use my precious life-energy
    Breathing out . . . Disguising the changes in my body and life.
Breathing in . . . My changing body is holy.
    Breathing out . . . There is no blemish.
Breathing in . . . With gratitude, I celebrate the accumulation
    Breathing out . . . Of my years and my wisdom.

6

Imagine a woman who has access to the full range of human emotion.

A woman who expresses her feelings clearly and directly.

Who allows them to pass through her as gracefully as a breath.

The Feeling
of the Universe

In the very beginning, the girl-child has the capacity to feel and to express the whole range of human emotion. The primary emotions create sensations and energy-tracks through her body. Through her body, she knows her feelings. Through movement and sound, she releases the energy, accompanying each feeling. No separation exists between her feelings and her body. They are one within her. She feels sadness as an ache in her heart and as the tears flowing from her eyes. She feels anger rise up within her and releases it in loud sounds and strong movements. She feels fear in the shortness of her breath and in the fluttering sensation in her tummy. She feels erotic energy in the tingling warmth of her genitals. She feels joy in the warmth of her face, the smile in her eyes, and in the giggle inside of her. Her feelings ebb and flow as naturally as the breath. When she gets angry, she stomps and yells, and before you know it, she's smiling and off with a friend. The expression of a full range of human emotion is essential to her physical and psychological health. Her immune system is strengthened by the circulation of her feelings. The feeling of the universe pulsate through her. She is in love with herself.

This capacity to feel, however, was judged as fickle, too intense, and inferior by our parents. Although we were allowed more room to feel than our brothers, an inherent judgment surrounded our capacity to feel. Feelings were not as important as thoughts. Boys think. Girls feel. Our feelings were tolerated at best and dismissed at worst as evidence of our inferiority. We heard rumors of women who allowed their feelings to keep them from getting a job done, unlike men who mastered their feelings and completed the task at hand; of women who were too emotional and good-for-nothing, especially at that time of the month, unlike men who could be counted on all the time; of women who were fickle, erratic, and unstable because they let their feelings get the best of them, unlike men who were reliable and controlled.

There were good feelings and bad feelings. Responsible for the reactions of others, we sorted through our feelings. Bad feelings were to be controlled and kept inside because they made others uncomfortable. Good feelings could be expressed as long as they weren't too intense. Intensity made everyone uncomfortable. We became aware of boy-feelings and girl-feelings. Girls got hurt and cried a lot. Boys got angry and yelled a lot. If a boy got hurt, he was called a sissy. If a girl got angry, she was called unfeminine and ugly. Humble, discreet, and considerate, we learned to cry when we were angry and to smile when we really wanted to yell.

The exploration and expression of a full range of human emotion is essential to physical and psychological health. Our immune systems are strengthened by an appropriate circulation of emotions on a daily basis. Most of us confuse our thoughts with our feelings. We are much more adept at conceptualizing our emotions—"I think I'm afraid of my boss"—than we are at noticing and then expressing the bodily sensations that reveal our emotions to us: "I notice a tightness in my abdomen whenever I'm around my boss." Our bodies are faithful, however, and as we return home to them and pay attention to their sensations and impulses, we reclaim the skillfulness we knew in the very beginning of our lives when our feelings danced through us as gracefully as a breath. As you travel through this week of your life, practice the healthy circulation of your emotions:

1. Take full responsibility for your own feelings by experiencing a full-feeling cycle as it passes through your body.

   Notice the feeling sensation and name its location in your body.

   "I feel an ache in my heart. I notice tingling in my genitals."

   "I notice a band of pressure across my chest. I feel fire rising in my neck."

   Breathe into the sensation until it passes.

2. Create a personal expression using images, movements, and/or sounds to give voice to the feeling. Become the feeling: Does it have a sound to make? Sound it! Does it want to move or dance through you? Move it! Does it have a color or shape? Color it!

3. Take action on the information you receive from your feelings. It is not always necessary to express your feelings to others. When

appropriate, however, circulation involves taking action without drama, blame, or shame. Ask yourself, "Did my feelings clarify the necessity of setting a limit, acknowledging a resentment, leaving a job, leaving a relationship, restructuring my life, or clearing up the past?"

Daughter of Woman, access the full range of human emotion.
Express your feelings clearly and directly.
Allow them to pass through you as gracefully as a breath.

The Heart of Life

According to Eastern teachings, the fourth chakra is the Heart Center. It is connected to our capacity to love, to open, and to give. There is an acupressure point located at the Heart Center on the sternum between your breasts. Place the fingertips of each hand there. This powerful acupressure point strengthens the blood and calms anxiety. The Chinese call it the "Sea of Tranquility" or the "Sea of Blood." Begin and end the day with the "Heart Center" meditation. As you become familiar with the movements, improvise and create your own meditation.

Breathe in with fingertips on sternum ... Heart of Life,
    Breathe out as arms open outward ... To you I am opening.

Breathe in, bringing fingertips to sternum ... Strong is your pulse,

Breathe out as arms open outward . . . Soothing is your touch.

Breathe in, bringing fingertips to sternum . . . In you,
    Breathe out as arms open outward . . . I feel, and flow, and live.

Breathe in with fingertips on sternum . . . Heart of Life,
    Breathe out as arms open outward . . . To you I open.

Breathe in, bringing fingertips to sternum . . . Steady is your pulse,
    Breathe out as arms open outward . . . Healing is your touch.

Breathe in, bringing fingertips to sternum . . . In you,
    Breathe out as arms open outward . . . I feel, and flow, and live.

The Gift of Feeling

Turn your attention inward by taking two deep breaths. Imagine standing in your favorite place in the natural world. Allow your bare feet to touch the earth. Take two more deep breaths.
Breathing in . . . The breath rises from the earth beneath me.
    Breathing out . . . I release the breath into the air around me.
Breathing in . . . I savor the breath of life
    Breathing out . . . As it flows in and through and around me.

A circle of benches appears. Find a place to sit in the middle of the circle. Your core emotions—sadness, anger, fear, arousal, and joy—

walk into the clearing and sit on the benches. When they are all seated, turn toward them one by one. In your journal, acknowledge the ways they teach, heal, and challenge you. For example:

> "Anger, you are my teacher. I have learned to speak the truth through acknowledging you."

> "Arousal, you are my healer. I have grown to know myself more deeply through acknowledging you."

> "Fear, you are my challenge. I have stretched beyond my comfort zone and developed untouched parts of myself through acknowledging you."

When you are finished acknowledging each core emotion, step outside the circle and view them across a loving distance. Conclude the meditation by chanting their names on each exhale.

Breathing in . . . Anger, rising up my middle.
Breathing out . . . Loud sounds and strong movements.
Breathing in . . . Anger,
Breathing out . . . I am grateful for your presence in my life.

Breathing in . . . Arousal, tingling warmth.
Breathing out . . . Pulsations of pleasure.
Breathing in . . . Arousal,
Breathing out . . . I am grateful for your presence in my life.

Breathing in . . . Fear, catching my breath.
Breathing out . . . Tightness in my belly.
Breathing in . . . Fear,
Breathing out . . . I am grateful for your presence in my life.

Breathing in . . . Joy, warm face.
Breathing out . . . Smiling eyes.
Breathing in . . . Joy,
Breathing out . . . I am grateful for your presence in my life.

Breathing in . . . Sadness, an ache in my heart.
Breathing out . . . A tear flowing from my eye.
Breathing in . . . Sadness,
Breathing out . . . I am grateful for your presence in my life.

Breathing in . . . I have access to the full range of human emotion.
Breathing out . . . I express my feelings clearly and directly.
Breathing in . . . I allow them to pass through me
Breathing out . . . As gracefully as a breath.

7

Imagine a woman who tells the truth.

A woman who trusts her experience of the world and expresses it.

Who refuses to defer to the thoughts, perceptions, and responses of others.

The Truth
of the Universe

In the very beginning, the girl-child tells the truth about what she thinks and how she responds to the events of life. She is transparent, forthright, and bold. When she doesn't like her food, she spits it out. When she's exhausted from tagging along on a shopping spree, she refuses to take another step. When she doesn't like someone, she tightens in their presence and makes her discomfort known. She has a mind of her own and responds to the events of life with her own set of opinions. She tells her mother, "I get tired when you stay at those meetings so late. Can't we leave earlier?" She tells her father, "I like it when you read stories with me in the morning." She confronts her parents, "When you fight with each other late at night, I hear your voices and it makes me sad and afraid. I wish you wouldn't fight." She tells the truth when she is asked questions:

"No, I don't like the new baby-sitter. She yells."

"No, I don't like to sit on uncle's lap."

"Yes, I want a room of my own."

The truth of the universe pulsates through her. She is in love with herself.

Eventually, our capacity to tell the truth was judged as rude and "not nice," and our capacity to think for ourselves as "troublesome" and "rocking the boat" by our families. We learned to question our own thoughts and perceptions and to lie in a compliance-based environment that valued conformity to gender stereotypes and "politeness" more than it valued originality and integrity. We kept our thoughts about the events of life to ourselves so there wouldn't be an argument. We strained to like everyone so we wouldn't hurt anyone's feelings. We pretended that we didn't know what we knew so their egos wouldn't be hurt; that we didn't hear what we heard so their secrets wouldn't be exposed; and that we couldn't do what we could do so the masquerade about who was weak and who was strong would be maintained. We were required to be nice and pleasant at the expense of our own healthy integrity. The constant repetition of these childhood commandments censored our natural tendency to tell the truth and to think for ourselves. Humble, discreet, and considerate, we learned to question our truth and to defer to the thoughts and perceptions of others, assuming something was wrong with us.

Reclaim your capacity to tell the truth by enlisting the transformational capacities of your imagination. Enter into the following "Healthy Family Fantasy" in the quietness of your imagination.

Your mother calls you and your sisters together for a family meeting. She begins with a reading from *The Book of Woman:* "For Mother God so loved the world that she sent into its midst the

Divine Girl-Child. Whosoever believes in Her goodness, listens to Her wisdom, and celebrates Her power will be awakened to the abundance of gifts within them."

"I have called this meeting to discuss a new job I have been offered. Whatever decision is made will affect all of us so I want to lay out the situation and hear your concerns." She then lists the benefits of the new job: Weekends off. Better health benefits. Paid two-week vacation. And then she lays out the challenges of the job: After-school care until 6 P.M. every day. Less time with her during the week. Long days for everyone from Monday to Friday.

Each of the children has a turn to express her opinion about the changes. You respond: "The kids are wild after school and I don't like to be around them for three hours. The child-care people are not as good with kids as the teachers. I'd rather go to Aunt Lucy's than stay at school." Your mother asks you how many days you can handle staying at school. "Three days," you say, "because there is drama class after school on Monday, Wednesday, and Friday and I like drama." "OK," Mom responds, "we'll call Aunt Lucy and see if she can pick you up on Tuesdays and Thursdays."

"I have two more problems. First, I get really hungry after school and the snack is not enough." Your mother asks, "Would it work for you to make two lunches for yourself on Monday, Wednesday, and Friday, and eat one after school?"

"Good idea. My other problem is that I want to be sure that we really do get to do fun things on the weekend when you are off. Not just laundry and stuff to clean up around the house." "OK," your mom responds, "Let's plan a date for every Saturday evening. We'll go roller-skating or we'll rent a movie. No chores or busyness on Saturday from 5 P.M. on. How's that?"

"Now that we've worked through all that stuff, I vote yes to your new job." Your mom thanks you for being so clear about what doesn't work for you. "It's fun to co-create solutions with you. You have great ideas and I can always count on you to tell me the truth about things even if it's a hard truth. Thank you!"

The images of a childhood hoped for vanish. Imagine the Mother of All Living turning toward you with these words . . .

"Daughter of Woman, tell the truth. Trust your experience of the world and express it. Refuse to defer to the thoughts, perceptions, and responses of others. Be sassy and loud. Question. Argue. Debate. Communicate from your heart. Voice your truth. When you don't like your food, spit it out. When you're exhausted from tagging along in someone else's life, refuse to take another step. When you don't like someone and tighten in their presence, make your discomfort known. Tell the untold truths of a lifetime to your parents, lovers, and colleagues, and to your children and grandchildren. The truth of the universe pulsates through you."

Telling Yourself the Truth

Truth-telling begins with ourselves. After each encounter with a new friend, colleague, or potential lover, pause to breathe deeply. In the silence, listen to yourself.

1. "What worked about our encounter?"

   Examples:

   He listens without an agenda.
   She's at home in the natural world.
   We shared equally in the planning and expenses of the day.
   There is absolutely no sexual pressure when we're together.
   Answer the question in your journal.

2. "What didn't work about our encounter?"

   Examples:

   He becomes defensive easily.
   Her moods fluctuate from high to low within a two-hour time period.
   I've stated my limits clearly and he continues to push sexually.
   He planned and financed the day and wouldn't allow me to participate.
   Answer the question in your journal.

3. Review past lists after each encounter. Notice if the things that work continue to work after a month. Notice if the things that don't work were circumstantial or if they develop into chronic "red flags." Trust your experience and express it.

Breathing in . . . My encounters are infused with consciousness.
Breathing out . . . I turn toward them with open eyes.

Telling Others the Truth

A woman who loves herself makes direct statements in response to
the requests of others, sets clear limits in her interactions with others,
and offers respectful solutions to her interpersonal challenges. With
courage and respect for her own life, she no longer hides her truth
within convoluted narratives and indirect explanations. Initially, her
use of the vocabulary of truth is awkward. Eventually, her responses
become graceful and effective.

1. Create two columns in your journal and list the interpersonal
   challenges you are facing. For example:

PERSON	NATURE OF CHALLENGE
My mother	She gives me advice. She won't just listen.
My boss	She disregards our agreements.
My lover	He calls late at night after my bedtime.

2. Read through the following examples of truth-telling. Highlight
   the ones relevant to your situation. Gather a truth-telling vocabulary to use in your particular interpersonal challenges.

A To a spouse who disapproves of partner's dress, music, or friends: "I will be considerate of your preferences when appropriate, but I am unwilling to eliminate those things that bring me pleasure."

B To a daughter who will not deal directly with her father: "I am no longer available as the go-between in conflicts with your father. I encourage you to speak to your father directly."

C To a mother who gives unsolicited advice: "I appreciate your concern for me, Mom, but I need to find my own way through this problem and would prefer that you just listen."

D To a sibling who is irritable in response to a change in the ground rules: "I am unwilling to give you advice anymore. I understand how uncomfortable this change is, yet it has been crucial to my emotional health to back off and allow you and others to find your own way without my interference."

E To a partner who complains daily about his job: "I cannot do anything to change your situation and it makes me crazy to hear you repeat this litany over and over again. Only you have the power to change your situation. Please limit what you tell me about it."

F To the family at the end of a day filled with intense interactions: "I need time alone to read and write for the rest of the evening. I am unavailable to anyone from this point on."

G To a neighbor who asks for a ride: "It will not work for me to give you a ride because my time is limited today."

H To a friend: "I don't enjoy our interactions. They are no longer supportive to me. I need some time away from the friendship. Let's touch base in a month to see if things have shifted for me."

I In response to an invitation: "Thank you for the invitation but that particular event does not interest me. I enjoy your company so let's find an activity of interest to both of us."

J In response to an employer's request: "I am unwilling to take on any more projects without additional compensation and a readjustment of my basic job description."

K In response to a friend's request to participate in his project: "I don't have the time to work with you now. My own projects demand all my energy and attention. At some point, a trade may work. Let's stay in touch."

I In response to a request to shift to a committed relationship: "I'm attracted to you and would like to date occasionally. I also want to date others, so a committed relationship is not possible at this time."

3. Reread your list of interpersonal challenges. Practice truth-telling with the support of the samples you've read. For example,

NATURE OF CHALLENGE	TRUTH-TELLING
My mother gives me advice.	C
My boss disregards our agreements.	J
My lover calls late at night.	"Please don't call me after ten."

4. Address one of your interpersonal challenges each week for the next month by writing a letter, making a phone call, or arranging a person-to-person encounter. Tell the simple truth!

Breathing in . . . I tell the truth
  Breathing out . . . To myself and to others.
Breathing in . . . I refuse to defer to the perceptions and responses of others.
  Breathing out . . . I trust my experience and express it.
Breathing in . . . I infuse my relationships with consciousness.
  Breathing out . . . I turn toward them with integrity.

8

Imagine a woman who follows her creative impulses.

A woman who produces original creations.

Who refuses to color inside someone else's lines.

The Originality
of the Universe

In the very beginning, the girl-child trusts her vision of the world and expresses it. With wonder and delight, she paints a picture, creates a dance, and makes up a song. Giving expression to her creative impulses is as natural to her as breathing. She creates in her own language, imagery, movement. She follows no script. She is not bound by the customary way things have been expressed. Her creative intuition is original. She gathers all of life into her inner crucible and mixes it with her unique vision and experience. She produces an original creation. She loves the sounds, movements, ideas, images, and words that emerge from inside of her. Sometimes the creative impulse leads her to share her dance, her song, her picture. She is full of herself as she performs before audiences large and small. Other times she does not want to share her creative expression with anyone. She reads to herself, creates an art showing in the privacy of her bedroom, or dances with her beloved stuffed bears as her audience. The originality of the universe pulsates through her. She is in love with herself.

So often our capacity to create was judged as impractical, not good enough, and "outside the lines" by our parents and teachers. Very early on, our creative expressions were exposed to the competition-oriented comments of well-meaning others who judged our work as "better than" or "not as good as." Perfection became the goal and anything less than perfect was thrown away. No longer was the emphasis on spontaneous expression rising from our own inner lives; product and performance took center stage. Creative expression became work assigned by parents and teachers with specific performance goals as its motivation. "Being creative" became a job to be done in its proper time and place. As our lives became cluttered with responsibility for others in the family and with the preoccupation with their needs, creativity became a scheduled task like everything else.

Eventually, we lost touch with the spontaneous expressions of our inner lives. There was a particular way things were to be done, and if we dared to use our own colors, shapes, or movements, or to experiment with a brand-new way of doing something, we were scolded for venturing outside the lines. Humble, discreet, and considerate, we learned to stifle our creative impulses except in service of the careers and projects of our children and lovers, our friends and colleagues. We learned to color inside someone else's lines.

Reclaim your creative originality by enlisting the transformational capacities of your imagination. Enter into the following "Healthy Family Fantasy" in the quietness of your healing imagination. Place your childhood name in the blank.

Sometimes your sister reads to you from the *Book of Woman*. One school night after you finish your homework, she offers to read a story to you. You ask her to read "_____'s Favorite Room."

For as long as _____ can remember, there has been a *whole* room in the apartments and houses she's lived in, filled with paint, crayons, glitter, and construction paper of all colors; glue, tape, stickers, and scissors of all kinds; sponges, brushes, and tongue depressors of all shapes; piles of old magazines, paper plates, and material scraps; containers of leaves and acorns, and other "found objects" from family walks and trips to the junkyard; a big table to work on; and large sheets of paper tacked up on all the walls, ready for the next adventure. Even when she lived in a very small apartment, her mom said, "What do we need a dining room for? We'll use it for our 'Play Womb' and eat in the kitchen. To create is the food of the soul."

"Play Womb" is what _____ 's mother calls the room because she believes that everyone can give birth to images, sounds, movements, and ideas—everyone, she said, even boys, have a "creative womb." Her father calls it the "Family Studio" because the room belongs to everyone in the family and "studio" sounded official to him—"we are all artists and everywhere we go, we will have a studio," he is always saying. And _____ calls it the "Play Room" because she has so much fun whenever she is in there.

A big sign is over the doorway. It says, "Be Full of Yourself!" A bowl of glitter is attached to the wall like the holy water containers in the Catholic Church. "This is our family church," her mom is always saying, "it is a holy place, so we'll bless ourselves with glitter before entering." So _____ reaches into the bowl and sprinkles herself with glitter every time she enters. There are only three rules in the playroom and they are easy to follow:

1. Cover the paints when you are finished using them for the day.

2. Be sure everything you use finds its way home to a pile, container, or shelf before you leave.

3. Move your painting to the "Drying Wall." Return for it within an hour. Hang it in the family gallery for public display or in your bedroom gallery for private display.

There is a sign-up sheet outside the "Play Room" so everyone in the family can spend private time in there each week. _____ always signs up for the after-school hours because she has lots to say after a long day, and she can't find the words to say it all—so she paints instead.

    One day after school, _____ was very upset when she entered her special room. She painted rows and rows of girls and boys, and put a big X through each of them while saying, "Go away." She painted twenty-five Xs and said twenty-five "Go away"s because there are twenty-five-plus children her in the class. She was tired of them all, talking, yelling, fighting, and spilling—she wished she could be the only person in her class. After she painted the twenty-fifth X and said the twenty-fifth "Go away," _____ felt a lot better. She covered the paints, washed her hands, and then went into the kitchen to say "Hi" to her father. No one in the family bothers _____ until she finishes her afternoon time in the Play Room. They know she'll be in a much better mood after spending time in there!

The images of a childhood hoped for vanish.

Imagine the Mother of All Living turning toward you with these words . . .

"Daughter of Woman, trust your vision of the world and express it. With wonder and delight, paint a picture, create a dance, and make up a song. Giving expression to your creative impulses is as natural as your breathing. Create in your own language, imagery, and movement. Follow no script. Be not bound by the customary way things have been expressed. Your creative intuition is original. Gather all of life into your inner crucible, mix it with your unique vision and experience, and produce an original creation. Refuse to color inside someone else's lines.

"Daughter of Woman, love the sounds, movements, ideas, images, and words emerging from inside of you. If the creative impulse leads you to share your dance, song, or picture; your design, quilt, or collage; your business, workshop, or sermon, be full of yourself as you 'perform' before audiences large and small. If you do not want to share your creative expression with anyone, read to yourself, create an art showing in the privacy of your bedroom, or dance with your beloved stuffed bears as your audience. The originality of the universe pulsates through you. Be full of yourself."

An Impulse to Move

Turn your attention inward by taking two deep breaths into your belly. Savor the breath of life as it journeys in, through, and around you. As you breathe deeply, turn toward your body. Place your hands on your belly and feel it expand and contract with the breath. Weave an affirmation into each breath:

Breathing in . . . I come home to the natural resources of my own life.
   Breathing out . . . Home is always waiting.

As you continue to breathe deeply, listen to your inner experience for impulses to move or to make a sound. The impulse may be as simple as the "urge" to move your little finger or as complex as the "whim" to get down on the floor in a fetal position. It may be as playful as the desire to become a land, sea, or air creature, or as cathartic as the release of a sigh, yawn, or scream.

Pay attention as the impulse builds inside of you. Allow the impulse to take form in a movement and/or a sound that expresses it fully. Notice when the impulse subsides and your expression is complete. Notice when your impulse shifts to another movement or sound.

If your attention moves away from your body and breath toward an external distraction, notice the distraction without judgment and practice returning home. Breathe again into this moment and listen for the impulses of your inner experience.

If your attention moves away from the expression of your natural impulses toward intellectual attempts to figure them out, reverse your tendency to interrupt pure expression by breathing again into this moment, reestablishing conscious contact with your inner experience. Home is always waiting.

When you experience a sense of completion, conclude the "Inner Listening" meditation by turning toward your body with gratitude. It communicates to you through impulses and sensations. Honor your body in the silence, weaving an affirmation into each breath:

Breathing in . . . I descend into the richness of my inner life.
  Breathing out . . . I express the treasures I discover there.
Breathing in . . . I come home
  Breathing out . . . To my body's impulses and sensations
Breathing in . . . To its movements and sounds.
  Breathing out . . . Home is always waiting.

Unfolding Images

Use an indoor or outdoor wall or a tabletop as your canvas. Tape newspaper onto the surface, and a large sheet of paper over it. Begin simply with a set of magic markers. As you are moved, gather luscious paints, tongue depressors, sponges, and paper plates on which to mix and experiment with color.

Turn your attention inward by taking two deep breaths into your belly. Savor the breath of life as it journeys in, through, and around you. As you breathe deeply, turn toward your body. Place your hands on your belly and feel it expand and contract with the breath. Weave an affirmation into each breath:

Breathing in . . . I come home to the natural resources of my own life.
    Breathing out . . . Home is always waiting.

As you continue to breathe deeply, scan your inner landscape for images. An inner image may appear as a simple line of color or as a complex image of a woman giving birth. It may be a playful impulse to paint stars across the canvas or a cathartic release of a disturbing dream image. Pay attention as the image forms within you. Allow an image or series of images to take form on the canvas or in your journal-sketchpad. Express them fully. Notice when the impulse subsides and your expression is complete. Notice when your impulse shifts to another image.

If your attention moves away from the expression of your images toward performance-oriented attempts to paint the perfect representation of an image, reverse your self-critical tendencies to interrupt spontaneous expression by breathing again into this moment, reestablishing conscious contact with your inner experience. Home is always waiting.

When you experience a sense of completion, step back from your painting and view it from a distance, asking, "What words dance with

the images?" and "What message does the image convey to me?"
Create a word-collage or poem to accompany your painting. Allow
words to spill onto the page without censorship.

Display your painting(s) in your creative space. Honor your images in
the silence. Affirm, *"Blessed is the fruit of my creative womb."* Descend
often into the richness of your inner life and express the treasures you
discover there. To conclude the meditation, weave an affirmation into
each breath:

Breathing in . . . I come home to the natural resources of my own life.
    Breathing out . . . I follow my creative impulses.
Breathing in . . . I produce original creations,
    Breathing out . . . Refusing to color inside someone else's lines.
Breathing in . . . I come home to the natural resources of my own life.
    Breathing out . . . Home is always waiting.

9

Imagine a woman who names her own gods.

A woman who imagines the divine in her image and likeness.

Who designs a personal spirituality to inform her daily life.

The Spirit
of the Universe

In the very beginning of her life, the girl-child has direct access to the spirit of life. It is as near to her as the breath that fills her. It connects her to everything. She is not alone. Her spirit is one with the spirit of her beloved grandmother, of her favorite rock, tree, and star. She develops her own special methods for contacting the spirit in all things.

She climbs a tree and sits in its branches, listening. She loves the woods and listens there, too. She has a special friend—a rock. She gives it a name and eats her lunch with it whenever she can. She keeps the window open next to her bed even on the coldest nights. She loves the fresh air on her face. She pulls the covers tight around her chin and listens to the mysterious night sky. She believes that her grand-mother is present even though everyone else says she is dead. Each night, she drapes the curtain over her shoulders for privacy, looks out the window near her bed, listens for Grandma, and then says silent prayers to her.

Her imagination is free for a time. She needs no priest or teacher to describe "God" to her. Spirit erupts spontaneously in colorful and unique expressions. God is Grandma, the twinkling evening star, the gentle breeze that washes across her face, the peaceful, quiet darkness after everyone has fallen asleep, and all the colors of the rainbow. Because she is a girl, her experience and expression of spirit is uniquely feminine. It flows from her essence as naturally as a breath. The spirit of the universe pulsates through her. She is in love with herself.

Eventually the girl-child will turn away from the Spirit-filled One she once was. Her original spirituality will become confined within the acceptable lines of religion. She will be taught the right way to imagine and name God. "He" will be mediated to her through words, images, stories, and myths shaped, written, and spoken by men. She will adopt the god she is given. It is too dangerous to rebel. If she dares to venture out of the lines, if she insists on communing with the spirit of a tree, the mysterious night sky, or her grandma, she will be labeled a heretic, a backslider, or a witch. She is told:

Prideful One,
Your grandma is not God; neither is your favorite star or rock.
God has only one name and one face.
    You shall have no gods before him.
God is Father, Son, and Holy Ghost. He is found in the church,
    in the heavens, in the holy book, not in you.
God is the God of Abraham, Isaac, and Jacob. He is God of the
    fathers and sons; the daughters have no say in the matter.
Remember:
    As it was in the beginning, it is now and ever shall be.

The Spirit-filled One falls asleep. Occasionally she awakens to remind the girl-child-turned-woman of what she once knew. These periodic reminders are painful. The woman fills her life with distractions so she will not hear the quiet inner voice, calling her to return home . . . to her own spirituality.

Years later, new teachers enter the woman's life—a therapist, a self-help group, a women's support circle, a beloved friend, or perhaps this book. They remind her of what she once knew:

↦ 92

Spirit-filled One,
Your grandma is God and so are your favorite star and rock.
   God has many names and many faces.
God is Mother, Daughter, and Wise Old Crone.
   She is found in your mothers, in your daughters, and in you.
God is the God of Sarah and Hagar, of Leah and Rachel.
   She is Mother of All Living, and blessed are her daughters.
You are girl-woman made in her image.
The spirit of the universe pulsates through you.
   Be full of yourself. You are good. You are very good.

Women are reclaiming the divine feminine today. Surrounded by women from every age and inspired by their courage, we are committing the forbidden acts of naming and imagining the gods of our understanding as Goddess, Woman God, and God the Mother. Although we are not all devotees of the Goddess, it has been essential for us to extend our historical and theological vision to include the divine feminine. Some find her within traditional religion in the images and stories of Eve and Mary, Sophia and Shekhinah, Miriam and Esther, Naomi and Ruth, Tamar and Susanna, and of countless unnamed women. They are incorporating these women's stories into their liturgies and prayers. Others find her on the margins of patriarchal history in the images and stories of the Goddess. They are incorporating her images into their paintings and songs, their altars and prayers, and they are weaving her ancient festivals and beliefs into their unfolding spirituality.

Inspired by a view of history that reaches beyond the beginning defined by men, women are assuming theological equality with religious traditions and reclaiming the richness of their own imaginations. We have come to believe that the theological tasks performed by men throughout the ages were not inspired by a god out there somewhere. Instead, they were prompted by a very human and natural inclination to answer existential questions and to order disparate experiences into a coherent whole through religious imagination. Humankind's religious imagination has always given birth to goddesses and gods and to stories making sense of our beginnings and endings. No longer held hostage by a truncated view of history or by the dominance of the Genesis account of creation, our imaginations are once again free.

Daughter of Woman, name your own gods.
Imagine the divine in your image and likeness.
Design a personal spirituality to inform your daily life.

The Changing Face of God

Imagine walking into church each Sabbath and being greeted by an image of the divine feminine above the altar and pulpit, in the stained glass windows, and in the storybooks read to you in Sunday School.

Imagine learning about her in sermons and church school lessons as the embodiment of the three aspects of a woman's life: Maiden, Mother, and Crone. Imagine encountering her in the depth of your being, knowing she is intimately acquainted with your woman-tears and laughter, your woman-dreams and desires, your woman-challenges and transitions.

Imagine learning a movement-blessing in acknowledgment of the three aspects of the divine, to be offered each time you stand before her image in the church, synagogue, or home of your childhood:

"In the name of the Mother of All Living,"
Touch your womb center in honor of the mother's intimate involvement in the origins of life.

"and of the Divine Daughter,"
Touch your breasts in honor of the daughter's developing body.

"and of the Wise Old Woman,"
Touch your eyes in honor of old woman's clear inner vision acquired through the accumulation of years.

"As it was in the very beginning, may it be now."
Open your arms to honor All That Is.

Breathing in . . . I name my own gods.
    Breathing out . . . I imagine the divine in my image and likeness.
Breathing in . . . I design a personal spirituality.
    Breathing out . . . It informs my daily life.

Bring Many Names

The ultimate truth, wisdom, and mystery of the Universe is far deeper, higher, wider, and richer than any name or image we use to capture it. Mystery cannot be confined within a language. Let us bring many names . . . and no names at all.

Bring many names . . . moving us beyond the limitations of gender:
Breathing in . . . Deeper Wisdom
    Breathing out . . . Source of Life
Breathing in . . . Community of Support
    Breathing out . . . Sacred Breath

Bring many names . . . retaining the relational quality of the divine:
Breathing in . . . Loving Wise One
    Breathing out . . . Welcoming Friend
Breathing in . . . Compassionate One
    Breathing out . . . Nurturing One

Bring many names . . . weaving traditional names into an unfolding spirituality:
Breathing in . . . Loving Father
    Breathing out . . . Abba
Breathing in . . . Wise Spirit
    Breathing out . . . Mother–Father God

Bring many names . . . challenging the idolatry of traditional religion:
Breathing in . . . Goddess
    Breathing out . . . Woman God
Breathing in . . . Sister God
    Breathing out . . . Sophia
Breathing in . . . A God with Breasts Like Mine
    Breathing out . . . Mother of All Living

Bring many names and no names at all . . . In the silence, let us leave space for the unknown.*Breathing in . . . In the silence,*
    Breathing out . . . I leave space for the unknown.

10

Imagine a woman who refuses to surrender to gods, gurus, and higher powers.

A woman who has descended into her own inner life.

Who asserts her will in harmony with its impulses and instincts.

The Wisdom
of the Universe

Sitting in a Twelve-Step meeting several years ago, I listened as a woman spoke about learning to trust the god of her understanding: "When I let my Higher Power take charge, everything works out fine. When I'm in the driver's seat, I blow it every time." Inspired by her talk, several other women acknowledged that they were fundamentally ill equipped to deal with life. Based on their sense of inadequacy, each one found it necessary to "surrender" to a power greater than themselves. Later that week, I sat in a women's support circle as a woman complained about the unavailability of her therapist who was on vacation: "I have to see her every week or things begin to fall apart around me. I don't seem to have what it takes to live my life without the assistance of a trained professional."

While on a book tour supporting *A God Who Looks Like Me*, I was interviewed on a religious radio show. During the call-in part of the program, the inevitable question about sin and salvation was asked: "Do you believe we are sinners and in need of the salvation God offers?" I told the caller that my own inner wisdom was trustworthy and that it was communicated to me through my natural impulses, instincts, and intuition. I no longer needed the salvation offered by gods, higher powers, therapists, or gurus. The caller was appalled. "We can't trust ourselves," she exclaimed, "we are sinful, and left to our own devices, we will mess things up every time. God is the only trustworthy one."

Convinced that our lives are not our own, we become alienated from our inner sense of what is true, right, and appropriate for us. We become experts at watching the way others live and we shape our lives accordingly. From talk show hosts to Ann Landers, from our therapists and trainers to the countless experts we consult to design our experience, everyone else knows better than we do. We have spent our lifetimes trying to fit into someone else's idea of what is right for us: assembling our bodies according to society's formula of the perfect woman, forming our thoughts and opinions to suit the audience, limiting our feelings to what's acceptable, and formulating our behavior and actions according to the expectations of others. We have become emotionally crippled as a result of habitually abandoning ourselves to fit into the shapes of others. Each surrender of our feelings, our truth, and our originality becomes a mini-abdication of who we are.

Reminded of the truth about ourselves, we reject the dominance of cultural and religious myths and theologies that exiled willful women, portraying us as powerless victims incapable of independent thought and action, self-determining choice, or the successful implementation of our desires in the world. We reject the passivity-based messages that require the surrender of our wills to the dictates of others. We embrace a woman-affirming perspective that reminds us of our original willfulness. We remember ancient women who valued their willfulness and who encouraged their daughters to believe their "will" was valid and achievable in the world. We remember ancient ways that taught women to refuse submission and subordination and applauded women for their assertiveness. Women who exerted, initiated, and moved on their own behalf in harmony with their own deep wisdom. Women in love with themselves!

Inspired by the stories of old, women are turning inward—instead of looking to a god or higher power outside of our lives for salvation, we journey "home" to ourselves. Instead of ascending to enlightened states of being that involve the denial of the self, we have discovered that ours is a journey of descent: we look deep within to reclaim forgotten aspects of ourselves. We reach beneath our obsession with flaws, beneath the accomplishments that mask our sense of unworthiness, beneath years of alienation from ourselves, toward the goodness at our center. We discover that the good is deeply embedded within us. As we embrace our original goodness, our inner spaces are cleared out and reclaimed as our own. We find rest within our own lives and accept all of ourselves as worthy.

In our descent, we rediscover Sophia, the Greek word for wisdom. She is a feminine aspect of the divine presented in the Hebrew scriptures. Her presence in the male pantheon of gods has been obscured but not completely eradicated. In the Gnostic writings, considered heretical by the "orthodox" church, Sophia was present at creation, for all things were conceived in feminine power and wisdom. After creation, she escorted Adam and Eve toward self-awareness. Women around the world are reclaiming Sophia as a representation of their own inner wisdom. No longer is "God's will" imposed from outside of their lives—wisdom unfolds from within them and is in sync with their own natural gifts and capacities. No longer available to turn their lives and wills over to gods, gurus, and experts, they are refusing to surrender, except to Wisdom's urgings. No longer abdicating responsibility for their lives, they are employing their own willfulness in harmony with Wisdom's ways.

Daughter of Woman, refuse to surrender to gods, gurus, and higher powers.
Descend into your own inner life.
Assert your will in harmony with its impulses and instincts.

Called by Many Names

A conscious life unfolds from the inside out. Your inner life has been called by many names and known by many images. Breathe into each name and image. Notice which one rings true for you.

Breathing in . . . Source of Life,
Breathing out . . . My life begins in you.

Breathing in . . . Ground of My Being,
  Breathing out . . . My life is rooted in you.
Breathing in . . . Deeper Wisdom,
  Breathing out . . . My life unfolds from you.
Breathing in . . . Truest Self,
  Breathing out . . . Integrity at the center of my being.
Breathing in . . . Heart Center,
  Breathing out . . . Compassion at the center of my being.
Breathing in . . . Womb Center,
  Breathing out . . . Creativity at the center of my being.
Breathing in . . . Inner Sanctuary,
  Breathing out . . . Stillness at the center of my being.
Breathing in . . . Sacred Clearing
  Breathing out . . . Spaciousness at the center of my being.
Breathing in . . . Intuition,
  Breathing out . . . Knowing at the center of my being.

Breathe deeply and discover your inner life.

Breathing in . . . I refuse to surrender to gods, gurus, and higher powers.
  Breathing out . . . I have descended into the rich resources of my own
    inner life.
Breathing in . . . I assert my will
  Breathing out . . . In harmony with its impulses and instincts.

An Encounter with Wisdom

Turn your attention inward by taking two deep breaths. Imagine standing in the clearing deep within the forest of your being. You are surrounded by ancient redwoods. Everything breathes in the forest. Take two more deep breaths.

Breathing in . . . The breath rises from the earth beneath me.
    Breathing out . . . I release the breath into the air around me.
Breathing in . . . I savor the breath of life
    Breathing out . . . As it flows in and through and around me.

A circle of benches appears. Sit on one of the benches. You are waiting for Wisdom to arrive. She may appear as someone you know: a wise teacher, grandmother, sister, or friend. Or Wisdom may visit as a mythic figure: the Wise Old Woman, the Mother of All Living, the Goddess, or the Divine Girl-Child.

In the fullness of time, Wisdom walks into the circle and sits across from you. Her eyes invite you to speak: "Tell me about the confusing situation, troubling relationship, disturbing memories, or current life challenge. Tell me about the situation consuming your thoughts." Remain in the quietness of your imagination while you describe your life challenge to her or write to her in your journal.

In the stillness following your presentation to her, ask Wisdom to answer a specific question about the situation you described or to offer a creative strategy for addressing your challenge. If an image forms, draw it. If a message wells up from the depths of you, write it down. Do not edit what comes. Simply write it down. When finished with your dialogue, thank Wisdom for her support.

To conclude the meditation, weave an affirmation into the breath:

Breathing in . . . I come home to the rich resources of my inner wisdom.
Breathing out . . . Home is always waiting.

II

Imagine a woman who is interested in her own life.

A woman who embraces her life as teacher, healer, and challenge.

Who is grateful for the ordinary moments of beauty and grace.

Ordinary Life
Is Interesting Enough

In the very beginning, the girl-child is interested in herself and involved in self-motivated adventures. She moves through each day with an exuberant strength, a remarkable energy, and a contagious liveliness. Every experience is filled with wonder and awe. It is enough to gaze at the redness of an apple, to watch the water flow over the rocks in a stream, to listen to the rain dance, to count the peas on her plate. She is a natural explorer of everything in her world. Life is her teacher, her challenge, and her delight. She is never bored. There is always another adventure and project to turn toward. Her ordinary life is interesting enough.

As she grows, this vitality dies. From her first reading of *Sleeping Beauty,* she longs to be delivered from ordinary life and transported to the realm of fairy-tales. She turns away from the Vital One she once was. Her intimate connection to life's unfolding is severed. No longer is ordinary life her challenge, inspiration, and delight; it is boring. She waits for a savior to come along and rescue her from "ordinary life."

She longs for human saviors: "if only" she had a different partner, job, or family; a life-changing insight or treatment; a big lottery win.

She longs for divine saviors: "if only" a vision from heaven, a miracle, a definite word from god/goddess/higher power through her therapist or guru. Her life remains on hold as she waits for the Deliverer to come. Eventually, she needs a drug of some sort—Prince Charming, alcohol, an adrenaline rush—to feel what she once felt spontaneously in the midst of her ordinary life.

Years later, wise teachers enter the woman's life: a therapist, women's circle, or beloved friend. They remind her of what she once knew: "Vital One, you move through life with an exuberant strength, a remarkable energy, and a contagious liveliness. Your ordinary life is interesting enough. It will be your challenge, inspiration, and delight. Embrace it with respect. Express it with all the colors of the rainbow. Trust its lessons above the prescriptions of experts. What you know is true. What you feel is real. What you see is there. Your ordinary life is good. It is very good."

As we heal into the present, we discover again what we once knew: ordinary life is interesting enough. And to our surprise, in the midst of working, playing, crying, laughing, and needing; while surrounded by red apples and spilt milk, vacuum cleaners and computers, ordinary women and men, dogs and cats and vets, and rivers that flow with water not wine, we encounter Gratitude.

Embrace your ordinary life, whatever its wrapping, for in the embrace you will hear the whisper of Gratitude. Listen for her in the ordinary activities of your day, in the ordinary encounters with loved ones, and in the ordinary challenges that rise to greet you each morning. She speaks from the depths of you, in the voice of your ordinary life.

Daughter of Woman, sustain interest in your own life.
Embrace it as your teacher, healer, and challenge.
Welcome its ordinary moments of beauty and grace with gratitude.

In Gratitude for the
Significant Others of Ordinary Life

Imagine standing in your favorite place in the natural world. Allow your bare feet to touch the earth. Feel the firm ground supporting you. A circle of benches appears. Sit in the middle of the circle and take two deep breaths. One by one your friends, relatives, and colleagues with whom you share ordinary life walk into the clearing and sit on the benches. List them in your journal as they enter.

When they are all seated, turn toward them one by one using the list as your guide. Acknowledge the ways they teach, heal, challenge, inspire, and delight you in your journal. For example:

"_____, you are my teacher. I have learned to speak the truth through knowing you."

"_____, you are my healer. I have grown to love myself more deeply through knowing you."

"_____, you are my challenge. I have stretched beyond my comfort zone through knowing you."

"_____, you are my inspiration. My choice for life is strengthened in your presence."

"_____, you are my delight. I have experienced joy through knowing you."

When you are finished acknowledging the significant others of your daily life, step outside the circle and view them across a loving distance. Write a poem, word-collage, or letter thanking each of them for teaching, healing, challenging, inspiring, or delighting you.

Conclude the meditation by weaving an affirmation into the breath.

Breathing in . . . (Visualize the person.)
  Breathing out . . . I am grateful for your presence in my life.

In Gratitude for the Activities of Ordinary Life

Imagine standing in your favorite place in the natural world. Allow your bare feet to touch the earth. Feel the firm ground supporting you. A circle of benches appears. Sit in the middle of the circle and take two deep breaths. One by one the everyday activities of your life walk into the clearing and sit on the benches. They may appear as a symbol, color, shape, or image representing the activity. List them in your journal as they enter. For example:

"Cooking breakfast every morning"

"Cutting fresh vegetables"

"Learning to use a computer"

"Reading a novel in bed"

When they are all seated, turn toward them one by one using the list as your guide. Acknowledge the ways they teach, heal, challenge, and delight you in your journal. For example:

"My teacher: Cutting fresh vegetables has opened my eyes to the earth's bounty."

"My healer: By cooking breakfast every morning, I have grown to accept my body's needs."

"My challenge: Learning to use a computer developed my unexplored capabilities."

"My delight: Reading a novel in bed at the end of a full day delights me."

When you are finished acknowledging the activities of your daily life, step outside the circle and view them across a loving distance. Write a poem or word-collage of gratitude dedicated to each activity, thanking it for teaching, healing, challenging, or delighting you.

Conclude the meditation by weaving an affirmation into the breath.

Breathing in . . . (Visualize the activity.)
Breathing out . . . I am grateful for your presence in my life.
Breathing in . . . I am interested in my own life.
Breathing out . . . I embrace it as my teacher, healer, and challenge.
Breathing in . . . With gratitude,
Breathing out . . . I welcome the ordinary moments of beauty and grace.

12

Imagine a woman who authors her own life.

A woman who trusts her inner sense of what is right for her.

Who refuses to twist her life out of shape to meet the expectations of others.

The Vocabulary
of Self-Possession

In the very beginning, the girl-child is self-possessed. She doesn't need experts to manage her movements, from crawling to walking to running; her sounds, from garbles to words to sentences; or her learning about the world through her amazing senses. Her own interests, curiosities, and capacities orchestrate the flow of her days. She sings songs to herself for an hour straight, loving her own company; she sits in the attic for a whole afternoon, looking through old picture albums while conversing with her dead grandmother; she ventures into the meadow beside her house in the morning and forgets all about lunch as she carries on important conversations with her favorite trees.

Inundated with cultural and religious myths elevating women who have relinquish the ownership of their bodies, the authorship of their lives, and the naming of their experience, the girl-child will enter adolescence questioning her ability to control her own destiny and to function independently in her own life. She will twist her body, life, and experience into the acceptable shapes of the culture. In the process, she loses touch with the shape-spinning center within her.

Years later, wise teachers enter the woman's life: a therapist, women's circle, or beloved friend. They remind her of ancient times when virginity meant being owned by no man, being the author of one's own life and the creator of one's own destiny. They remind her of ancient women who refused to surrender the ownership of their bodies except to their natural rhythms and cycles. Women who refused to surrender the authorship of their lives except to their deepest wisdom. Women who refused to surrender the naming of their experience except to their inner truth. Women full of themselves!

Reminded of the truth about ourselves, we relearn the vocabulary of self-possession. It replaces the dependency-based vocabulary of our socialization and our chronic tendency to abdicate our lives to the design and specifications of others. Consider the following examples of the vocabulary of self-possession. Highlight the ones that resonate with your own experience. Incorporate the vocabulary of self-possession into your daily conversations, interactions, and challenges.

1. From a self-possessed center, we speak to ourselves with strength:

    "My body is my own. I will not allow the standards of others to twist it out of shape. My thoughts are my own. I will not allow them to be molded by others. My feelings are my own. I will not allow them to be expressed by others. My life is my own. I will not allow it to be shaped by the expectations of others. I refuse to surrender my self-possession to the dictates and specifications of others. I will live in harmony with my natural rhythms and cycles, my deepest wisdom, and my truest self. I am full of myself!"

2. From a self-possessed center, we author our own lives with strength. Our first question when faced with a life challenge is, "What inner resources do I have to address this challenge?" We begin by consulting our own feelings, thoughts, intuition, and bodily sensations. They will escort us on the journey toward a creative solution:

   ◦ "I notice that I become irritated in the presence of a colleague. Clearly the irritation is mine. I'll take responsibility for it and get to know it before I dump it on her. I'll begin by paying attention to the feelings and thoughts that pass through me when I'm in her office next week."

   ◦ "I notice a growing sexual attraction to my daughter's teacher. It's my attraction and I wonder what it's telling me about myself. I'll take responsibility for it by paying special attention to my body and its sexual needs this week."

3. From a self-possessed center, we refuse to embrace any set of principles based on the belief in our fundamental sinfulness and defectiveness, or on the necessity of ego-deflation, humiliation, or the surrender of our natural impulses. Instead, we reframe them to reflect our commitment to self-celebration.

   Women are rewriting the Twelve Steps based on their belief in original goodness. Each step now answers the question, "What's good and right about us?" and affirms our natural impulse toward healing and wholeness:

↬ Step 1 as written: We admitted we were powerless over alcohol—that our lives had become unmanageable.

↬ Step 1 as rewritten: I do not have all the resources I need to deal with my alcoholism. I have reached out for help to AA. This was a brave action on my own behalf. I celebrate my courage today.

↬ Step 8 as written: Made a list of all persons we had harmed, and become willing to make amends to them all.

↬ Step 8 as rewritten: I will make a list of all persons I have hurt in my life and all persons I have helped. I will take responsibility for my ineffective behaviors that have hurt others. I will celebrate my life-affirming behaviors that have supported others even in the most overwhelming moments of my addiction.

4. From a self-possessed center, we refuse to participate in a pathology-based therapeutic process. When choosing an advocate to support us through life's challenges, we interview therapists carefully to determine if they're willing to co-create woman-affirming solutions and strategies.

↬ She/he recognizes the historical, political, intellectual, and religious context within which women's lives are shaped, and acknowledges these systemic realities while addressing the current challenge.

◦ She/he moves beyond insight and information to facilitate a woman's reconnection to her body and breath, and to her rich inner resources of creativity and wisdom.

◦ She/he supports a woman's journey from passive dependence on experts to trust in her own inner wisdom; from over-responsibility for the lives of others to action on her own behalf; from self-criticism to self-celebration; and from personal recovery to healing action in the world.

Daughter of Woman, author your own life.
Trust your inner sense of what is right for you.
Refuse to twist your life out of shape to meet the expectations of others.

The Full Emptiness

Twisted into the shapes of experts, of family expectations, of job descriptions, we lose touch with our feelings, our thoughts, and the shape-spinning center within us. All who are aching, come. Courage awaits you here. Rediscover the shape of your life.

Noticing Clutter

Imagine your life as a house. How many rooms are in your house? In your journal, draw a house with that many rooms. Name the rooms. For example: Work. Community Involvement. Hobbies. Significant Relationships. Political Action. Place a star in your four favorite rooms. What do you like about them?

Walk into each room and notice how you feel. Is the room cluttered or spacious? Can you walk around in it? Is there space to dance, draw, and write? Can you breathe deeply in the room? Are you aware of your body and its needs in the room?

A Shape-Spinning Center

Imagine discovering an empty room in the center of your house. This is your shape-spinning center. From it, the shape of your life is spun. It is unfurnished . . . empty, yet full.

Walk into the room. Sit in the middle of it. Observe the size of the room, the shape of the windows, the light and the shadows. Note the specifics of this empty yet full room. Redraw your house. This time include the room you have discovered at the center of the house.

Uncomfortable with the room's emptiness, you wonder aloud, "How will the room be furnished?" An answer comes, "Run to the furniture store. From its mass-produced stock, the room will be filled!" As you imagine the room furnished in this way, it groans loudly and silences the suggestion.

The full-emptiness speaks to you: "Do not fill your house with mass-produced furniture. It will be creatively furnished from your own life. This process will take time. Each furnishing will be carefully fashioned. Each experience of your life will be woven into the unfolding design of your home's furnishings."

Recognizing the wisdom of the full-emptiness, you ask: "Have I brought any mass-produced furniture into the house of my life?" Travel again through each room of your house. This time pay attention to the contents of the room. Invite the full-emptiness to groan if any furniture in the room has been imposed from mass-produced stock. Note the groan in some way.

Design your life from the inside out. Ask for the ongoing support of the full-emptiness, "Groan loudly if I bring any activity, attitude, job, person, or experience into my life that does not flow from my shape-spinning center, that is not creatively fashioned from my own life, that is not in harmony with my own deep wisdom. I will listen to your groan."

Breathing in . . . My life is infused with consciousness.
Breathing out . . . I trust my inner sense of what's right for me.

A Calendar of Support

Rediscover the shape of your daily life. Divide a sheet of 8½-by-14-inch paper into seven columns. Label the columns, beginning with Monday and ending with Sunday. Gather color markers.

Personal Commitments

Design a life in which you turn toward yourself regularly. Choose a color to represent your personal commitments. Using that color marker, place the givens of your personal life on the calendar. Include meals, sleep, exercise, personal hobbies, spiritual practice, and creative projects.

Family Commitments

Design a life in which you turn toward your loved ones regularly. Choose a color to represent your family commitments. Using that color marker, place the givens of your family life on the calendar. Include time with partner and children, household chores and responsibilities.

↜ 121

Social Commitments

Design a life in which you turn toward those who make you smile regularly. Choose a color to represent your social commitments. Using that color marker, place the givens of your social life on the calendar. Include time with individual friends, regular social engagements, and the maintenance of long-distance relationships.

Work Commitments

Design a life in which your natural gifts and capacities are utilized. Choose a color to represent your work commitments. Using that color marker, shade in the time you spend at work, including regular evening meetings and work at home.

Community Commitments

Design a life that honors your interconnectedness with the extended human community. Choose a color to represent your community commitments. Using that color marker, place the givens of your community life on the calendar, including church attendance, political involvement, and club memberships.

Open Spaces

Leave space for the unknown. Notice if there are any open spaces on your calendar. Is your tendency to fill each empty space? Consider including an hour of open space in each day, an evening of open space in each week, a day of open space in each month. What feelings come up as you simply consider this suggestion? Honor the open spaces by choosing a color or symbol to represent the spaciousness of your life. Outline the open spaces on your calendar and leave them empty.

Breathing in . . . I infuse the details of my life with consciousness.
Breathing out . . . I author my own life.

13

Imagine a woman who participates in her own life.

A woman who meets each challenge with creativity.

Who takes action on her own behalf with clarity and strength.

The Vocabulary
of Willfulness

In the very beginning, the girl-child is a warrior. She is capable of carrying out any task that confronts her. She has everything she needs within the grasp of her mind and imagination. She accomplishes great things in the neighborhood, in her room, and in her mind. Whatever the challenge, she knows there is a way to deal with it. It takes no effort for her to summon up her courage, to arouse her spirit. With her courage, she solves problems. With her spirit, she changes what doesn't work for her. She says no when she doesn't want to be hugged. She says yes when she wants to spend time with folks who love, respect, and listen to her. She takes care of herself.

There are those who are threatened by the girl-child's willfulness. Whether well-meaning or abusive, they will attempt to preach it out of her. She is told, "Stubborn and angry one, don't be so proud and uppity. Say yes when you mean no. Give your anger to god. Pretend you don't know what you know. Pretend you can't do what you can do. Ask the boys to help you. The world's a big and scary place for Little Red Riding Hood. Eve's daughters are small, weak, and powerless." Eventually, the willful one falls asleep. Occasionally she awakens to remind the woman of what she once knew. These periodic reminders are painful. The woman fills her life with distractions so she will not hear the quiet inner voice calling her to return home . . . to her own willfulness, power, and courage.

Years later, wise teachers enter the woman's life: a therapist, women's circle, or beloved friend. They remind her of what she once knew in the very beginning of her life, and she learns again the vocabulary of willfulness. It replaces the passivity-based vocabulary fed to us since childhood. No longer waiting for a deliverer to come, we take responsibility to implement our desires in the world. No longer accepting spectator status, we choose to participate fully in our lives. Consider the following examples of the vocabulary of willfulness. Highlight the ones that resonate with your own experience. Incorporate the vocabulary of willfulness into your daily conversations, interactions, and challenges.

1. No longer asking, "What's wrong with me?" we change what isn't working and celebrate what is. Supported by our willfulness, we take action in our own behalf by acknowledging what works for us and going after it, and by acknowledging what doesn't work for us and changing it. We speak to ourselves with courage, incorporating self-celebratory affirmations into our inner dialogues:

   "I am capable of carrying out any task that confronts me. I have everything I need within the grasp of my mind and imagination. I accomplish great things in my home, neighborhood, and world.

Whatever the challenge, I know there is a way to deal with it. It takes no effort for me to summon up my courage, to arouse my spirit. With my courage, I solve problems. With my spirit, I change what doesn't work for me. I've reclaimed my own willfulness. I am capable of independent thought and action, of self-determining choice, and of the successful implementation of my desires in the world. I exert, initiate, and move in my own behalf."

2. No longer accepting depression as a fact of our existence, we regularly inventory our lives to notice what's working and what isn't. Calling upon our inner and outer support systems, we change what we can and let go of what we can't.

- "It's not working for me to eat dinners alone. I will invite my unpartnered friends to share meals with me three times a week, possibly rotating to each other's homes."

- "My job is depleting me. I refuse to use my precious life-energy complaining about what isn't working. I will speak to my boss and arrange for a four-day work week. This will free up an extra day for my creative projects while the kids are in school."

- "My apartment is cluttered with the stuff of the past. Every time I walk into it, I cringe. I will spend this weekend sorting and cleaning. I will hire the neighbor kid to help once I've brought some order to the mess. When completed, I will invite my women's group over to bless the apartment's new life."

3. No longer settling for relationships that don't work, we regularly evaluate them, express our concerns, and invite participation in the co-creation of solutions that work for us.

  ↪ "I am no longer willing to reach out to you on a regular basis unless you meet me halfway. I am unavailable for relationships that are not mutual. If you value our time together, please call and make the arrangements for our next get-together."

  ↪ "I am unavailable to hear another litany of complaints about your marriage. If and when you become ready to co-create solutions or to take action in your own behalf, I will gladly listen. Until then, let's talk about other areas of interest for the two of us."

↪ 127

  ↪ "I am no longer available to support you through your current life challenge. You broke two of our agreements: you did not call me concerning your Al-Anon commitment and you did not call to cancel your Monday session. When you are ready to act with integrity in your own behalf, give me a call."

  ↪ "This is the third time you've been late to pick the kids up for the weekend. Out of respect for the children's anticipation of your arrival and in recognition of the importance of my week-end plans, I ask you to redesign your Friday afternoons. Or arrange for a friend or colleague to pick the children up and bring them to your office. If it happens again, we must sit down with a mediator and co-create a solution that works for all of us."

↜ "My life is full at this time. I do not have the time or energy to engage in these daily conversations. It works for me to check in weekly. And I encourage you to extend your circle of support to include others who can be there for you on a daily basis."

↜ "My financial resources are limited. I'm saving for a house for me and my children. I'm unable to lend you the money you need. I encourage you to address the underlying concerns which have created your financial vulnerability. Here's a meeting schedule for Debtors Anonymous groups in the area."

↜ "Given the shifts in my schedule, it no longer works for me to prepare dinner every evening. I would appreciate sharing that responsibility with you. I can handle it on Tuesday, Thursday, and the weekend. Will you cook the other nights? Or should we hire a cook?"

4. When choosing an advocate to support us through life's challenges, we interview therapists carefully to determine if they have developed a collaborative mentality.

↜ "I am contracting your services to support me through a current life challenge. I will participate fully in our sessions to co-create strategies with which to address this challenge. If at any point our collaboration does not work for either of us, we will reevaluate our contract and dissolve it if necessary."

Daughter of Woman, participate in your own life.
Meet each challenge with creativity.
Act on your own behalf with clarity and strength.

Settle into the Moment

The breath will escort you into this moment. Life becomes simpler, clearer, and lighter as you settle into this moment. You have everything you need to be here . . . now. Breathe into the fullness of this moment with each inhalation. With each exhalation, release past moments that will never be again and future moments that may never be.

Breathing in . . . I acknowledge this moment.
  Breathing out . . . I let go of the past: an hour, day, year, or decade ago.
Breathing in . . . I enter into this moment.
  Breathing out . . . I let go of _____. (Name specifics of the past that are distracting you from this moment.)

Breathing in . . . I acknowledge this moment.
  Breathing out . . . I let go of the future: an hour, day, year, or decade from now.
Breathing in . . . I enter into this moment.
  Breathing out . . . I let go of _____. (Name specifics of the future that are distracting you from this moment.)

Breathing in . . . I choose to participate fully in this moment.
Breathing out . . . I have all that I need to be here, now.

Gathering Support

Imagine standing in your favorite place in the natural world. Allow your bare feet to touch the earth. A circle of benches appears. Sit on one of the benches. You are waiting for your closest friends to arrive. In the fullness of time, they walk into the circle one by one. Once they have gathered, sit in silence together. Synchronize your breath with theirs.

Turn toward them one by one and remember the ways they have supported you during the years. Remember the ways you have supported them. Weave an affirmation into the breath:

Breathing in . . . I acknowledge my circle of supportive friends.
Breathing out . . . With gratitude, I remember them.

↭ In your journal, list the ways you have supported your friends through the years.

Examples: Provided child care so a friend could train for a job. Prepared daily dinners for a friend after her surgery. Lent sister money so she could leave abusive marriage. Organized weekly circle to support friend during her first pregnancy.

↭ List the ways your friends have supported you through the years.

Examples: Daily visits while I was in the hospital. Regular feedback on book drafts. Massages when I hurt my shoulder. A life-challenge circle to brainstorm solutions.

- Describe your current life challenges.

Examples: Raising money for my child's education. Simplifying my weekly schedule so there is time for self-care. Creating a responsible financial life. Completing a creative project. Deciding whether to leave a depleting job and marriage.

- There are many points in our lives when we need extra support. Acknowledge your particular support needs during a challenging season by personalizing the following list of support options. Highlight the options that fit your current situation and then add your own.

Gathering Self-Care Support

- A daily phone conversation with _____ to circulate the feelings associated with the life challenge.

- A weekly matinee date with _____ to counteract my tendency to obsess about the challenge.

- An evening walk to gain perspective by viewing the challenge against the expansiveness of the night sky.

- Weekly postcards of encouragement from _____.

+ Supportive messages left on the machine by _____.

Gathering Brainstorming Support
+ A brainstorming session with _____, _____, _____, and _____ to develop creative solutions to deal with the challenge.

Gathering Project Support
+ A daily project check-in with _____ to declare each day's work commitment and then a regular check-in with her machine to report my progress.

Gathering Decision-Making Support
+ A clarity session with _____, _____, _____, and _____ to support my decision-making process and gain a variety of perspectives by considering their insightful questions and their helpful feedback.

+ Create a calendar of support for yourself. Review the list of support options. Schedule as many of them as possible into the next month.

   + I will guard the time from _____ to _____ on Monday through Thursday for a walk. (Place the days and times of your walks on the calendar.)

   + I will arrange a daily phone conversation with my closest friend to circulate the feelings associated with the life challenge. (Place the time on the calendar.)

↪ I will pass the calendar around my life-challenge circle and mothers' group to see who is available to send a weekly post-card of encouragement, to leave supportive messages on my machine, and to go to a weekly matinee. (Place the weekly matinee date on the calendar.)

↪ I will call _____, _____, and _____ to schedule the brain-storming session. (Place the date and time of session on the calendar.)

↪ I will call _____, _____, and _____ to schedule the clarity session. (Place the date and time of session on the calendar.)

↪ I will discuss the "project buddy" option with _____ because she is also working on a project. The daily check-ins may be mutually supportive. (Place the time of morning check-ins on the calendar.)

Breathing in . . . I participate in my own life.
    Breathing out . . . I meet each challenge with creativity.
Breathing in . . . My challenges are infused with consciousness.
    Breathing out . . . I gather the support I need to address them.

14

Imagine a woman who has crafted a fully formed solitude.

A woman who is available to herself.

Who chooses friends and lovers with the capacity to respect her solitude.

The Blessing
of Solitude

In the very beginning, the girl-child enjoys the privacy of quiet times, under-the-cover times, alone times to digest the events and experiences of her life. She is always available to herself so she is never really alone. She keeps some things to herself, holding them in the privacy of her own heart. She has a new idea that's too fragile to share so she keeps it close to her. If she tells someone about it too soon, the fragile blossom may wilt from premature exposure. She has a new friend who's too new to invite into her very private dreams; theirs is still too fragile a connection to hold the fullness of who she is. She has a new relationship with her body as it changes from day to day. She needs private time to befriend each change before she exposes her body to others. She loves the quiet of the night when everything slows down and she has a chance to think about the day, to feel the sadness in her heart, to let her imagination drift to other worlds, to see the dancing images of her night-dreams—all by herself. The solitude of the universe pulsates through her. She is in love with herself.

Our natural need for privacy was judged as selfish and unhelpful.

We watched our mother closely and learned that she had no private, under-the-covers, all-by-herself time except maybe in the bathroom but even there, someone was always barging in with a question or an emergency. Someone was always barging into our lives too. Barging in on our thoughts: "What are you thinking, young lady?" Barging in on our feelings: "Why so sad today?" Barging in on our rooms: "The guests will stay in your room for the week. You will have to move into your sister's room." Barging in on our time: "I need mama's helper to babysit your little brother today." Barging in on our bodies: "Come and sit on my lap, pretty girl." There was always someone barging in on our privacy with demands to help in the kitchen or to fix our little sister's hair. Our brother wasn't "on call" like we were. There were long stretches of time when he had nothing to do except what he wanted to do. His time was his own. Our time belonged to others. We were required to be helpful at the expense of our own healthy need for private time and space. The constant repetition of this childhood commandment censored our natural desire for solitude. Sometimes we felt like screaming, "Leave me alone!" Helpful and compliant, we swallowed those words and twisted our natural introversion into a much more acceptable and helper-oriented extroversion.

It is essential for women to reclaim and befriend their original solitude. A woman's choice to be alone, whether for an hour a day, a weekend a month, or for a full season of life, deepens her love for herself. In her solitude, she reclaims her abundant inner resources, nurtures her original creative spirit, reconnects with her own spontaneity and joy, and remembers her personal dreams and goals. The words of Rainer Maria Rilke, Anne Morrow Lindbergh, and Elizabeth Cady Stanton support us as we reclaim our solitude:

- ❧ "We are solitary. We may delude ourselves and act as though it were not so. But how much better it is to realize that we are so, yes, even to begin by assuming it. Naturally, we will turn giddy." (Rainer Maria Rilke, *Letters to a Young Poet*)

- ❧ "Instead of planting our solitude with our own dream blossoms, we choke the space with continuous music, chatter, and companionship. When the noise stops, there is no inner music to take its place. We must relearn to be alone." (Anne Morrow Lindbergh, *Gifts from the Sea*)

- ❧ "No matter how much women prefer to lean, to be protected and supported, nor how much men desire to have them do so, they must make the voyage of life alone, and for safety in an emergency, they must know something of the laws of navigation. To guide our own craft, we must be captain, pilot, engineer; with chart and compass to stand at the wheel; to watch the winds and waves, and know when to take in the sail, and to read the signs in the firmament over all. It matters not whether the solitary voyager is man or woman; nature, having endowed them equally, leaves them to their own skill and judgment in the hour of danger, and, if not equal to the occasion, alike they perish." (Elizabeth Cady Stanton, "The Solitude of Self")

For fifteen years, I have invited women to craft a fully formed solitude and to choose friends and lovers who have the capacity to respect, honor, and protect their solitude. In choosing the way of shared independence, friends, lovers, and partners see themselves as separate individuals, unique in feeling, thinking, and experience; each bringing a rich and colorful solitude to their friendship, partnership, or marriage. They become the guardians of each other's solitude. I spoke these words at a recent wedding:

> Times of aloneness are essential to the health of a relationship. Institute times of personal retreat early in your partnership lest you become deluded that you cannot survive without the other—even for a weekend. Don't become imprisoned by your affection. Keep your solitude.
>
> Guard the distance between you. Refuse to allow your lover to slip into your shadow. Lovingly support her to stay connected to the distinctiveness of who she is. Remind him of the beauty of his solitude. At times, the distance may seem unbridgeable. In these moments, too, you must guard the distance. You must leave the distance alone. In the fullness of time, you will make your way back to each other. You will find a place to meet. You will touch again. A distance born of love holds within it exquisite gifts for your relationship.
>
> Guard the differences between you. To love is to allow what is different to exist and to be itself. To love is to accept the otherness of the beloved. To love is to refuse to violate the mystery of the

beloved. Delight in each other's individuality, in the distinct shape of her thoughts, of his feelings, of each other's unique experience of life. Honor the boundaries that define your unique individuality. Say clear "Yes"s and "No"s to each other. Yes, you will bump into each other's borders. Yes, you will hurt each other. Learn to say "Ouch." And learn to make amends for trespassing.

Daughter of Woman, craft a fully formed solitude.
Be available to yourself.
Choose friends and lovers with the capacity to respect your solitude.

Out of Balance

Craft an enriching solitude (or review an already established solitude) by writing an inventory of the specific activities, attitudes, foods, and relationships that give shape to your life. Infuse your life-choices with consciousness, letting go of depletion and imbalance, and choosing nourishment and balance.

Certain activities, attitudes, foods, and persons support the cultivation of an unconscious life. They draw us away from our center. They throw us off-balance. They deplete the soul. Acknowledge the "centrifugal forces" that propel you away from your grounding center and inner life by personalizing the following list. Underline the "forces" that resonate with your own experience and then in your journal, add your own.

Activities

Every moment is filled up with something to do

Saying "Yes" when I want to say "No"

Fantasizing about men and sex

Shopping for stuff I don't need

Going anywhere during traffic time

Shopping on Saturdays

Isolating myself in my bedroom with a bag of chips

Too much time on the phone

Obsessive financial planning

Vegging out in front of the TV

Rushing in the morning

Working compulsively

Add your own.

Attitudes/Thinking

Comparing myself to others

Getting lost in the false logic of my anxiety

Hysterical ruminations about loss and disintegration

Obsessions about my body: clothing, appearance, aging, and physical condition

Obsessing about what others think of me
Swirling thoughts about the future
Add your own.

Foods and Substances

Eating in the car and on the run
Bingeing
Ice cream
Brownies
Sugar
Not eating regularly
Alcohol
Cookies
Pizza
Coffee
Add your own.

Persons

Coworkers who gossip
Relatives coming to visit
Listening to a friend's dating dramas
Spending time with my mother
Listening to victim-oriented friends

Talking on the phone to my sister
Add your own.

Using your calendar of support as a guide, calculate how much time you spend weekly in activities, attitudes, foods, substances, and relationships that deplete you. Cross out the "centrifugal forces" you will let go of during the next six months.

Breathing in . . . My choices are infused with consciousness.
Breathing out . . . I let go of depletion and imbalance.

In Balance

Certain activities, attitudes, environments, foods, and persons support us to remain faithful to our own lives. They draw us toward our center. They support inner and outer harmony and balance. They nourish the soul. Acknowledge the "centripetal forces" that draw you toward your grounding center and inner life by personalizing the following list. Underline the "forces" that resonate with your own experience and then in your journal, add your own.

Activities
Creating a painting or collage
Moving my body consciously

Doing stretching exercises

Organizing my finances

Grocery shopping on regular basis

Saying "No" to a request

Listening to classical music

Speaking the truth

Listening to inspirational music

Swimming laps

Add your own.

Foods

A light dinner of soup and salad

Home-made soup with fresh-baked bread

Brown rice and vegetables

Simple foods

Fresh steamed vegetables

Unhurried eating

Fresh fruit for breakfast

Vegetarian meals

Add your own.

People

An hour of "special time" with each of my kids weekly

Daily phone contact with a trusted friend

Laughing with my children

Regular conversations with non-shaming relatives

Sharing my inner experience with my therapist

Spontaneous times of affection with my partner

Weekly tea with my best friend

Add your own.

In the Natural World

Being in quiet and uninhabited places

Smelling the flowers in my garden

Birding

Visits to the desert

Feeling the sun on my face

Walks along the shore

Hiking in the mountains

Walks in the forest

Nighttime walks when the moon is full

Watching the sun set

Add your own.

At Home

    Free time with nothing planned
    Rocking in my rocking chair
    Quiet time in my home
    Sipping a cup of jasmine tea
    Quilting after everyone is in bed
    Time in my garden every day
    Reading in bed
    Walking my dog every evening
    Reading to my children at bedtime
    Writing in my journal
    Add your own.

Recovery Practices

    Attending Twelve-Step meetings
    Repeating the slogans
    Making program calls
    Saying the serenity prayer
    Reading the daily meditation book
    Spending time with recovery friends
    Remembering the first three steps

Weekly meetings with my sponsor
Add your own.

Spiritual Practices

Attending outdoor church services

Silent meditation in a group

Cooking breakfast at a women's shelter

Singing in the church choir

My daily yoga routine

Spiritual workshops and retreats

Prayer and meditation

Volunteering at the local hospice

Add your own.

Craft an enriching solitude. Using your calendar of support as a guide, weave the experiences that nourish your soul and support consciousness in your life. Turn toward two of the above "centripetal forces" every day of the next week.

Breathing in . . . I have crafted a fully formed solitude.
  Breathing out . . . I am available to myself.
Breathing in . . . My choices are infused with consciousness.
  Breathing out . . . I choose nourishment and balance.

15

Imagine a woman who refuses to diminish her life so others will feel better.

A woman who brings the fullness of her years, experience, and wisdom into each relationship.

Who expects others to be challenged and blessed by her presence in their lives.

The Radiance
of the Universe

In the very beginning, the girl-child wants to be seen and acknowledged. She feels good around people who look her in the eye, who ask her questions about her life, and who listen to her answers. She can tell when someone *really* sees and hears and likes her. To be around someone like that feels like eating her favorite flavor of ice cream. She smiles from her head to her toes. The girl-child only shows her projects to the special people in her life, the ones who make her smile. She tells them about her special dreams, except the very private ones, and lets them know about most of her special adventures. She loves it when they say: "WOW, you're fantastic!" Or "That's a colorful picture you drew. I like to look at it." Or "Your body is so very strong." Or "I'm so glad you are in my life!" Their words feel warm like the sun calling her out to play on a summer day. Their words say what she knows is true. She is a special girl: fantastic and strong and the maker of color-filled pictures and fun to be around. The radiance of the universe pulsates through her. She is in love with herself.

Our desire for acknowledgment was judged as conceited, big-headed, self-inflated, and pompous by our families. Daily, we walked through a minefield of warnings and admonitions to be humble about our projects, dreams, accomplishments, and adventures, and to be humble and quiet about ourselves at the expense of our own healthy self-celebration: "Don't be so egotistical and full of yourself. Don't blow your own horn. Don't brag. Pretend you don't know what you know so you won't hurt his ego. Do well quietly so others won't feel intimidated by you. Don't be so obvious with your talents. Don't hurt other people's feelings by being so good at everything. You're too big for your britches. Stop showing off. Who do you think you are? Pride goeth before a fall." The constant repetition of these childhood commandments censored our natural desire for acknowledgment and recognition. We were required to be quiet about ourselves, to pretend that our ideas, projects, dreams, and talents were small and inconsequential so we wouldn't hurt other people's feelings and so we would be liked. Humble, discreet, and considerate, we learned that girls are suppose to applaud for others, especially boys.

Reclaim your original fullness by enlisting the transformational capacities of your imagination. Enter into the following "Healthy Family Fantasy" in the quietness of your healing imagination. Place your childhood name in the blank.

Sometimes your mother reads to you from the *Book of Woman*. One school night after you finish your homework, she offers to read a story to you. You ask her to read "Show-and-Tell," and so she does.

One Saturday night a month, all of _____'s friends and the friends of her parents are invited over for "Show-and-Tell." _____'s mother is usually the Queen of Ceremonies because she always wanted to be a comedienne but her parents wanted her to learn to type until she got married. She didn't listen to her parents, never learned to type, and is the official comedienne of the family, the neighborhood, and the PTA. She starts off with the same words and actions every month:

"Be full of yourself.
Brag, boast, and show off.
Be pompous and big-headed.
Blow your own horn." (She blows a horn and passes it around!)

"Be loud about what you can do.
Be too big for your britches.
Have your cake and eat it too."
(She cuts the cake and passes it around!)

"Everyone gets a standing ovation because it takes courage to show-and-tell in front of an audience. Sometimes it takes more courage for us grown-ups to sing and dance, to share our ideas, and to read our words, but we do it and we get a standing ovation too. Let's practice the ovation before we begin." (Up and down until she thinks they've got it!)

One Saturday night, _____ was ready to sing her favorite country and western song. She had been practicing all week even though she knew the words by heart since she was four years old. She was the first one introduced by her mother and stepped onto the stage as her sister started the tape. At just the right moment she began to sing (with Nancy Griffith's help) "Love at the Five and Dime." _____ invited every one to join in at the chorus.

_____ got a standing ovation. At school they tell _____ that she "doesn't have a voice." She knows this isn't true. She does too have a voice and she hears herself use it everyday. And _____ loves to sing. It makes her smile deep inside. So she doesn't listen to the people at school who tell her those things about her voice. She listens to her friends and family. She loves it when they say, "WOW, you're fantastic!" Or "That's a great song you taught us. I sang it all week." Or "Your face sparkles when you sing." Or "I'm so glad you are in my life!" Their words feel warm like the sun calling her out to play on a summer day. Their words say what she knows is true. She is a special girl with a special voice and she'll keep singing because it makes her smile!

The images of a childhood hoped for vanish. Imagine the Mother of All Living turning toward you with these words . . .

"Daughter of woman, refuse to diminish your life so others will feel better. Bring the fullness of your years, experience, and wisdom into each relationship. Expect others to be touched, challenged, and changed by your presence in their life. Imagine into being a community of advocates—a chosen family available to nurture your deepening connection to yourself and to applaud your fullness. It is right and good that you are Woman. The radiance of the universe pulsates through you. Be full of yourself!"

Bite into Your Life

Imagine hearing Eve, the Mother of All Living, introduce the communion service one Sabbath morning: "As the Mother of All Living, I pick the fruit of life. It is good and satisfies hunger. It is pleasant to the eye and offers pleasure. It is wise and opens the way to self-discovery and understanding. Those among you who are curious, who lust for life in all its fluidity, dare with me. Bite into life. Eat of the fullness of its possibility."

After Eve speaks, the elder women of the congregation give an apple to the first person in each pew. As the crone hands you an apple, she looks into your eyes and says, "Take and eat of the good fruit of life. You are good. You are very good." You bite into the apple and savor its sweet juiciness, and then you pass it on to the person next to you with the same words.

After you have partaken of the good fruit of life, the Mother of All Living approaches you, bearing a multicolored jewel in her hands. She carries it into the darkness of your heart of hearts. The jewel illuminates the many facets of your stunning goodness and giftedness as a Child of Life. Imagine her saying to you: "Open to the depths of goodness within you. You are good. Celebrate your goodness. You are very good. Live out of the abundance of who you are as a Child of Life. You have everything you need."

Breathing in . . . I am opening to the depths of goodness within me.
   Breathing out . . . I believe in my goodness.
Breathing in . . . I live out of the abundance of who I am as a Child of Life.
   Breathing out . . . I celebrate my goodness.
Breathing in . . . I affirm the original goodness of my children.
   Breathing out . . . Until the stories of old hold no power in their hearts.
Breathing in . . . I will bite into my life
   Breathing in . . . And the fullness of its possibility.

The Party

The Guest List

Write a guest list to an imaginary party. Include the friends, colleagues, and relatives with whom you interact regularly.

The Party

All of the guests have arrived. They are gathered in one room. Walk around the room. Using your guest list as a guide, notice whom you are drawn toward and whom you wish to avoid. Now stop to look into the eyes of each guest.

   ⊸ In whose presence do you smile? In whose presence do you feel creative and energized? Place a smile next to their names on the guest list.

⤏ In whose presence do you become small? In whose presence does your stomach feel tight? Place a frown next to their names on the guest list.

A New Guest List

⤏ Place all of the friends, colleagues, and family members who delight you onto a new guest list. Write or phone each of them, sharing your gratitude for their presence in your life. Ask for regular contact: tea once a week, a walk once a month, a daily phone conversation. Choose to spend regular time with those who make you smile, those who nurture your deepening connection to yourself and applaud your fullness.

⤏ Place all of the guests who do not delight you onto another list. Consider limiting your contact with them. They are depleting your precious life-energy. Within the next month, set a contact-limit with each of them without shaming, blaming, or making them wrong.

Breathing in . . . I refuse to diminish my life
 Breathing out . . . So others will feel better.
Breathing in . . . I bring the fullness of who I am into each relationship.
 Breathing out . . . Others are challenged and blessed by my presence in their lives.
Breathing in . . . I infuse my relationships with consciousness.
 Breathing out . . . I turn toward them ith clarity.

16

Imagine a woman who assumes equality in her relationships.

A woman who no longer believes she is inferior to men and in need of their salvation.

Who has taken her rightful place beside them in the human community.

The Vocabulary
of Equality

In the very beginning, the girl-child recognizes no limits on her capacities and possibilities. She loves her body, feels her feelings, speaks her truth, expresses her creative spirit, and trusts her inner wisdom. There is nothing she cannot do: she joins the boys in their games, excels in the classroom, and helps her mom with the chores. The sky is the limit as far as her possibilities are concerned. She wants to pitch in the neighborhood baseball game, to be Peter Pan in the school play, and someday be President of the United States.

There are those who are threatened by the girl-child's capacities. Whether well-meaning or abusive, they will attempt to preach them out of her. She is told, "Tomboy, only boys can run fast, play hard, and climb trees. Only boys can be a pitcher, Peter Pan, President, and God. Be beautiful. Act coy. Strength, wit, and ability are reserved for the boys. No girls allowed. World without end. Amen." Eventually, her capacities will fall asleep within her. Occasionally they awaken to remind her of what she once knew. These periodic reminders are painful. She fills her life with distractions so she will not hear the quiet inner voice calling her to return home . . . to her own capacities.

Years later, wise teachers enter the woman's life: a therapist, women's circle, or beloved friend. They remind her of what she once knew in the very beginning of life and she relearns the vocabulary of equality. It replaces the hierarchically based vocabulary we learned in childhood and the exclusive language that continues to be used in every arena of life. Through our use of the language of equality, we step into our rightful place beside men. We assume equality in our personal and professional relationships, in the church, home, and world, and employ the full range of astounding capacities. Consider the following examples of the vocabulary of equality. Highlight the ones that resonate with your own experience. Incorporate the vocabulary of equality into your daily conversations, interactions, and challenges.

1. We speak to ourselves with self-respect, incorporating self-celebratory affirmations into our inner dialogues:

   "I celebrate the birth of my daughters, granddaughters, and nieces as I celebrate my own. I believe in their goodness as I believe in my own. I nurture their wisdom as I nurture my own. I cultivate their power as I cultivate my own. We are mothers and daughters, nieces and aunts, girls and women full of ourselves!"

2. We step into our rightful place in the human community.

   "I now know it is possible to have healthy and mutual relationships with men. And this is not because the male dominance of the world is changing. My vision of what is possible is transforming as I develop a loving and respectful relationship with myself. I no longer hate myself. I no longer believe that I am inferior. I walk into every encounter as a whole person expecting respect and mutual enhancement."

3. We are no longer available for relationships based on a one-up, one-down mentality in which men's interests take priority. We assume mutuality. We speak our mind and expect our intimate partners, friends, and associates to listen and acknowledge our thoughts, ideas, and concerns. We express our feelings and expect others to witness them without invalidating how we feel.

   ↬ "I have a full life today that includes special friends, personal projects, and compelling interests. I don't have time to elevate anyone to god status."

   ↬ "I'm an active participant in work situations. I celebrate the skills I bring to the workplace. I work with men as partners. I'm no longer intimidated by their intelligence."

   ↬ "Arguments are no longer my style of communication. Arguments involve a winner and a loser. I engage in healthy interactions today. We each present our concerns or issues. Then our challenge is to discover a way in which we both win for the greater good of the relationship."

4. Inspired by Simone de Beauvoir's words in *The Second Sex*, we articulate our commitment to the essential task of designing relationships of equality within our families.

- "We will bring up our daughters from the first with the same demands and rewards, the same severity and the same freedom, as their brothers, taking part in the same studies, the same games, and promised the same future."

- "As partners, we will assume on the same basis the material and moral responsibility of our children. The mother will enjoy the same lasting respect, responsibility, economic freedom, and prestige as the father."

- "We will orient our daughters toward their power and courage, authorizing them to test their powers in work and sports. We will instill into our sons a sense of equality, not superiority. They will be encouraged by the example of their father to look up to women with as much respect as they do men."

- "We will surround our children with women and men who are undoubted equals. They will perceive around them a world of equality in which both women and men have access to the full range of their human capacities."

- "We will surround our children with images of strong women so our daughters will be proud of themselves and our sons will learn to respect a woman's wholeness. We will surround our children with art, music, poetry, and books by and about women. They will hear of men's accomplishments in the wider world. In our home, women's voices and stories will be heard and respected."

5. We challenge exclusive language whenever it is spoken and wherever it is written. We choose to alleviate the persistent imbalance of voices bombarding us daily in newspapers, magazines, and textbooks; sermons and lectures; and in the "official" opinions and perspectives of our Western culture. For example, women and men are actively writing letters to magazines and newspapers to express their outrage at the continued use of exclusive language. I wrote the following letter to the editor of *Life* magazine regarding the article "Who Is God" in the December 1990 issue:

> In the introduction to your article, you assign the Supreme Being a gender through the use of that ever-present male pronoun, along with your choice of a picture of god as an old white man with a beard. This image has dominated the imaginations and self-concepts of men and women for centuries. Our imaginations have been held hostage by god the father. The "grandest of human imagination" will most certainly come up with a plurality of faces to inhabit the heavens, and with names that move us beyond the limitations of an exclusively white male god.

6. We refuse to participate in hierarchically based religious communities. We include ourselves by offering alternatives to the exclusive language and imagery used in religious liturgy, hymns, and sermons. We reverse the historic neglect of women's contributions and concerns by telling our stories.

   ↝ In a letter to each of the ministers, priests, and rabbis in the community:

"I am seeking a woman-affirming spiritual community in which my daughter's birth will be welcomed with as much pomp, circumstance, and opportunity as her brother's; where her body and its processes will not exclude her from participation in religious rituals; and where she will be surrounded by images of a god who looks like her in the presence of clergywomen and women priests. Is yours such a community?"

⊸ On a sermon-response card:

"Although I appreciate your congregation's apparent commitment to social justice, I've been disturbed by your sermons. You use quotations extensively to bolster your theme, yet no woman has ever been quoted. You clarify each point by telling a story from everyday life, yet not one story has included a woman, mother, or daughter. It is understandable that you gather experiences, stories, and quotations based on your male view of the world. I invite you however, to extend your vision to include women in order to more effectively minister to over half of your congregation."

⊸ 163

Daughter of Woman, assume equality in your relationships.
Relinquish the belief that you are inferior to men and in need of their salvation.
Take your rightful place beside them in the human community.

Parenting Inventory

Consider the following "Commitment to Equality." Celebrate the ways in which you have already incorporated equality into the parenting of your children ("strengths") and acknowledge the challenges you face in creating a household of equality ("challenges").

1. We will bring up our daughters from the first with the same demands and rewards, the same severity and the same freedom as their brothers, taking part in the same studies, the same games, and promised the same future.

   ↬ In your journal, celebrate your strengths in this area.

   ↬ In your journal, acknowledge the challenges you face.

2. As parenting partners, we will assume on the same basis the material and moral responsibility of our children. The mother will enjoy the same lasting respect, responsibility, economic freedom, and prestige as the father.

   ↬ In your journal, celebrate your strengths in this area.

   ↬ In your journal, acknowledge the challenges you face.

3. We will orient our daughters toward their power and courage, authorizing them to test their powers in work and sports.

   ↬ In your journal, celebrate your strengths in this area.

☞ In your journal, acknowledge the challenges you face.

4. We will instill into our sons a sense of equality, not superiority. They will be encouraged by the example of their father to look up to women with as much respect as they look up to men.

   ☞ In your journal, celebrate your strengths in this area.

   ☞ In your journal, acknowledge the challenges you face.

5. We will surround our children with women and men who are undoubted equals. They will perceive around them a world of equality in which both women and men have access to the full range of their human capacities.

   ☞ In your journal, celebrate your strengths in this area.

   ☞ In your journal, acknowledge the challenges you face.

6. We will surround our children with images of strong women so our daughters will be proud of themselves and our sons will learn to respect a woman's wholeness. We will surround our children with art, music, poetry, and books by and about women. They will hear of men's accomplishments in the wider world. In our home, women's voices and stories will be heard and respected.

   ☞ In your journal, celebrate your strengths in this area.

   ☞ In your journal, acknowledge the challenges you face.

Breathing in . . . I celebrate the birth of my daughters and granddaughters.
  Breathing out . . . As I celebrate my own.
Breathing in . . . I believe in their goodness
  Breathing out . . . As I believe in my own.
Breathing in . . . I nurture their wisdom
  Breathing out . . . As I nurture my own.
Breathing in . . . I cultivate their power
  Breathing out . . . As I cultivate my own.
Breathing in . . . We are mothers, daughters, nieces, aunts, girls, and women
  Breathing out . . . Full of ourselves!

Relationship Inventory

Consider the following "Commitment to Equality." Celebrate the ways in which you have already incorporated equality into your relationships ("strengths") and acknowledge the challenges you face in creating relationships of equality ("challenges").

1. I am an active participant in work situations. I celebrate the talents and skills I bring to the workplace. I work with men as partners. I am no longer intimidated by their presence and intelligence.

    ❧ In your journal, celebrate your strengths in this area.

    ❧ In your journal, acknowledge the challenges you face.

2. Arguments are no longer my style of communication. Arguments involve a winner and a loser. I engage in healthy interactions today. We each present our concerns or issues. Then our challenge is to discover a way in which we both win for the greater good of the relationship.

   ⤷ In your journal, celebrate your strengths in this area.

   ⤷ In your journal, acknowledge the challenges you face.

3. I enjoy the quality of my life, thoughts, and interests. I bring this enjoyment of myself into mixed groups of women and men. I expect to be heard with respect. I expect others to be enlarged in their perspective as a result of encountering me.

   ⤷ In your journal, celebrate your strengths in this area.

   ⤷ In your journal, acknowledge the challenges you face.

4. In mixed groups, I look into the eyes of women to acknowledge their presence. I listen to the stories and concerns of women. I ask women questions rather than defer to the men in the group.

   ⤷ In your journal, celebrate your strengths in this area.

   ⤷ In your journal, acknowledge the challenges you face.

5. I refuse to diminish my life so that others will feel better. I design peer relationships, bringing 100 percent of who I am into each exchange.

∾ In your journal, celebrate your strengths in this area.

∾ In your journal, acknowledge the challenges you face in this area.

6. My own life is most important today. I expect men to take care of their own emotional and spiritual needs in the company of other men. I no longer service them. I expect them to bring fullness rather than emptiness to our relationships.

∾ In your journal, celebrate your strengths in this area.

∾ In your journal, acknowledge the challenges you face.

Assume equality and expect mutuality in your relationships. Transform them from depleting to nourishing, from one-sided to reciprocal, from awkward to graceful, and from resentful to truthful.

Breathing in . . . I infuse my relationships with consciousness.
Breathing out . . . I turn toward them with equality and mutuality.

17

Imagine a woman who refuses to use her precious life-energy managing crisis and conflict.

A woman whose relationships deepen in satisfaction and contentment without depleting her.

Who chooses friends and lovers with the necessary skills to navigate through the challenges of life.

The Vocabulary
of Partnership

In the very beginning, the girl-child's body tells her everything she needs to know, including whether she likes someone or she doesn't. Whenever her grandmother is coming over to visit, her heart feels warm and her breath goes all the way down into her belly. One day, her mother brought over a new friend. As soon as he walked into their apartment, the girl-child's stomach got really tight and said, "I don't like him." She whispered, "Thanks for telling me, Stomach." From that day on she kept her distance from him. To be around someone like that feels like eating lima beans. Lima beans are a pretty color and shape and lots of grown-ups like them, but she doesn't. Just like it's OK that she doesn't like certain foods, it's OK that she doesn't like *everybody*.

Our natural-selection instincts were judged as rude and selfish. We were told, "Be nice. Nice girls get along with everyone. Nice girls don't say 'No.' Nice girls include others in their adventures. Nice girls don't hurt the feelings of others. Nice girls work hard to make relationships work." The essential connection to our intuitive body-centered wisdom was severed. We strained to like everyone so we wouldn't hurt anyone's feelings. We twisted our feelings, thoughts, and healthy self-interest out of shape to make relationships work, assuming any problem was our fault. We learned to put up with chronic crisis and conflict, forever hopeful that things would eventually work out if only we tried hard enough.

Reminded of the truth about ourselves, we reconnect to our bodies and their deep wisdom. We listen to the sensations of a lifetime: what they tell us about the quality of our lives, about the shape and pace of our days, and about our responses to those who dance into and out of our lives. Our eyes are open. Our senses are engaged. From a place of fullness, we look, sense, and determine what works for us and what doesn't. Our choices are wiser today because we trust what we see and what we sense; we trust our own "deeper wisdom."

A woman who is in love with herself refuses to use her precious life energy managing crisis and conflict. Instead, she chooses graceful relationships that deepen in satisfaction and contentment without depleting her. She chooses friends and partners who are willing to develop the relationship skills necessary to dance gracefully through life's challenging moments. Friends and partners who take responsibility for their own emotional, spiritual, and practical needs; who have a wide circle of support and maintain it. The historic "battle between the sexes" ceases. There is a willingness to find new ways of relating . . . as creative, business, or life partners, rather than enemies. Challenges have become opportunities to co-create solutions rather than excuses to blame or shame each other.

Clearly, our personal healing is only the beginning of the journey.

The ultimate salvation of the world depends upon developing a new kind of balance in which women and men offer their combined strength, wisdom, and compassion in service to humankind. As each partnership, whether composed of colleagues, friends, or lovers, finds its way to a sacred meeting place beyond right and wrong, beyond blaming and shaming, beyond one-up and one-down, the world becomes a safer, saner place for all of us. I invite colleagues, friends, and lovers to personalize the following commitment and affirmation in ways appropriate for them, and to incorporate the vocabulary of partnership into their discussions and meditations.

Our Commitment to Each Other

I respect the distance placed between us. You are a unique reality. I will not confine you within my formulas and definitions. You are an unfathomable mystery. I will not try to figure you out. You are a free person. I will not seek to possess you. Your journey is sacred. I will not judge or tamper with it. I will guard and protect your solitude. I will honor your boundaries. I will greet you often in the sacred garden we plant together along the fertile borders of our solitude.

An Affirmation of Our Partnership

We are partners. Together, we call upon the Deeper Wisdom to help us find our way through each issue that will cause us frustration, to help us find a middle space between our inevitable differences, to help us find a sacred meeting place beyond right or wrong.

Together, we trust the Deeper Wisdom to show us a way in which we will both win, a way that is comfortable for both of us, a way that will bring us both greater healing and joy. May our partnership flourish, one day at a time.

Daughter of Woman, refuse to use your precious life-energy
managing crisis and conflict.
Cultivate relationships that deepen in satisfaction and contentment
without depleting you.
Choose friends and lovers with the necessary skills to navigate
through the challenges of life.

A Breath Prayer

Turn your attention inward by taking two deep breaths. Imagine standing in a clearing deep within the forest of your being. You are surrounded by ancient redwoods. Everything breathes in the forest. Take two more deep breaths.

Breathing in . . . The breath rises from the rich earth beneath me.
Breathing out . . . The breath releases into the moist air around me.
Breathing in . . . I savor the breath of life
Breathing out . . . As it flows in and through and around me.

A circle of benches appear in the clearing. Sit in the middle of the circle. Your loved ones process into the clearing and sit on the benches. When they are all seated, turn toward them one by one.

Breathing in . . . (Name the person.)
    Breathing out . . . I am grateful for your presence in my life.
Breathing in . . . You are a free person.
    Breathing out . . . I will not seek to possess you.
Breathing in . . . You are a unique person.
    Breathing out . . . I will not try to figure you out.
Breathing in . . . Your journey is sacred.
    Breathing out . . . I will not judge or tamper with it.
Breathing in . . . Be well, _____.
    Breathing out . . . I am grateful for your presence in my life.

At the Stream of Living Water

Turn your attention inward by taking two deep breaths. Descend into the clearing surrounded by a sparkling stream of living water. Sit quietly on its bank and watch the faithfully flowing water. Become one with the flow. Breath into it.

Breathing in . . . I let go
    Breathing out . . . Into the wise flow of life.

The stream of living water reminds us that we are limited and finite. That there are some things we cannot change no matter how hard we try; no matter how desperately we want to rescue, fix, or work things out; no matter how genuine our concern or profound our love. There are some burdens we were not meant to carry: The life-choices of a loved one. The moodiness of a friend. The addiction of a coworker. The struggle of an adolescent. The depression of a relative. The changing nature of life. The twists and turns of the past. The unknown of the future.

It is deeply wise to lay down these burdens, to let them go into the stream of living water, to release them into the flow of life. As you are reminded of a situation, concern, person, or relationship you cannot change, let it go into the stream, naming it in the quietness of your heart. Be relieved of burdens that are not yours to carry.

Breathing in . . . I release _____
    Breathing out . . . Into the wise flow of life.
Breathing in . . . I release _____
    Breathing out . . . Into the wise flow of life.

As we let go of our futile attempts to change those things we cannot change, an abundance of energy is available to turn toward those things we *can* change. Ours is always a twofold acknowledgment. Yes, we are limited and finite. *And* we are powerful and gifted. There are many things we can change.

The stream invites you to step into full responsibility for your life. Courage is available to exert, initiate, and move on your own behalf in your relationships, in your workplace, and in the world. Reach into the stream and receive courage to change the things you can, naming them in the privacy of your own heart: To design your own life. To focus on a long-ignored creative interest. To author your own relationships. To end an energy-depleting friendship. To name your own gods. To take responsibility for your ineffective behaviors.

Breathing in . . . I receive the courage to _____
 Breathing out . . . I will act on my own behalf.
Breathing in . . . I receive the courage to _____
 Breathing out . . . I will act on my own behalf.

Conclude your meditation by weaving an affirmation into the breath:
Breathing in . . . I have everything I need
 Breathing out . . . To let go of depleting relationships.
Breathing in . . . I have everything I need
 Breathing out . . . To choose satisfying relationships.
Breathing in . . . I have everything I need
 Breathing out . . . Within the rich resources of my inner life.

18

Imagine a woman who values the women in her life.

A woman who sits in circles of women.

Who is reminded of the truth about herself when she forgets.

The Vocabulary
of Connection

Competition among women is woven into the fabric of a society that prefers men. We compete with each other for the attention of men. Inundated with cultural and religious attitudes fostering rivalry and suspicion among women, we lose touch with our original connection to the women in our lives. They function merely as fill-in companions between boyfriends. Inundated with homophobic messages, we become even more deeply alienated from each other and from the organic resources available in women-centered relationships. Like the steady drip of an IV inserted at birth, we absorb attitudes and fears designed to keep us separate.

At some point in our lives, most likely when we're reeling from another relationship failure, we reach out to a woman therapist, author, minister, or friend. Our original connection and solidarity with all women past, present, and future is reawakened. We begin to trust women, to know and be known by them, and to relax in their presence. They become the feminine face of god to us. As the face of god changes in our experience, we are reminded of the community of women that reaches back to a time when women valued each other, when they sat in circles to tell their stories and to remind each other of the truth. Tired of swirling around men, we begin to spend more time in the company of women. In each other's presence, the tears of a lifetime are shed, the forgotten stories are remembered and spoken aloud, and our former dignity and power as women are reclaimed.

Reminded of the truth about ourselves, we relearn the vocabulary of connection. It replaces the competition- and separation-based vocabulary we learn in a society that revolves around men. It supports us to define our own relationships. It reaffirms our primary connection to women as we embrace our primary connection to ourselves. Consider the following examples of the vocabulary of connection. Highlight the ones that resonate with your own experience. Incorporate the vocabulary of connection into your daily conversations, interactions, and challenges.

1. We speak to ourselves with integrity, incorporating self-celebratory affirmations into our inner dialogues:

   "I am developing intimate and honest relationships with beautiful, powerful, intelligent, and spiritual women. I no longer see them as a threat. They are a part of me and together we all become beautiful and strong. I am learning to love women as I learn to love myself."

2. We take responsibility for our competitive attitudes and behaviors by acknowledging the women we have been jealous of, gossiped about, called names or slandered, and competed with for the attention of a man. We become willing to make amends by changing our behaviors.

"I will make amends for my competitive attitudes by strengthening my relationships with women and giving them support rather than focusing on receiving the approval of men at work and in other settings. My colleagues and I are struggling to keep from feeling inferior to men so we compete with each other for their attention. I will make amends by learning to express appreciation and support, and by affirming our solidarity as women."

3. We spend more time in the company of women and less time swirling around men. Women are no longer just fill-in companions between our relationships. They are the ground of our support.

> ✦ "The community of women abides with me, comforts me, and provides me with a kind of security that a male lover can never do. The point is that I am a woman. The struggles and triumphs that other women experience as they go through life can guide and inform me as only women can."

> ✦ "As my connections with women have grown, my relationship with my partner occupies a smaller place in my life. My partner no longer dominates my life, thoughts, and feelings. He has diminished in significance and in psychological size. I am clearer. I have my own life. I can do things completely apart from him. I make my own decisions. I know what I think and feel. My relationship has changed so much. It's a new and different organism."

4. We no longer turn primarily to men to meet our needs or to answer our questions. Many of our emotional, spiritual, and intellectual needs are now met by women.

> ↬ "In the past, I expected my partner to take care of my feelings and to always be present for me. I don't have these expectations any more. He's just one thread in a big tapestry of support that surrounds my life. There are many times when I feel anxious or upset, or when I need to think an issue through with someone, and I don't go to him. I'm happy to go to the women in my life. I share with them my challenges and my celebrations."

> ↬ "Before being in a women's community, I wasn't aware of how strongly my search for truth was influenced by the male images of God. Nor was I aware of how these images invalidated me as a woman. It had never occurred to me to look toward a nurturing, strong, and feminine image of the divine. I've realized *at last* that what women offer is far more in alignment with what I've been seeking. Now I'm drawn to articles, books, and films written by women that deal with women's spiritual quests."

Daughter of woman, value the women in your life.
In the company of women,
You will be reminded of the truth about yourself when you forget.

The Womb Prayer

Imagine standing in a womb-circle with a group of trusted women: mythic figures who inspire you, teachers and relatives who loved you in your early years, and friends who support you today. Create a collage or draw a picture of this powerful circle of women. Display it as a reminder of the support available to you daily.

The Gifts of the Nurturing Womb

Do you desire the gifts of the nurturing womb: To sit and rest for awhile; to have your wounds caressed and your dreams held tenderly; to cry on a shoulder; to accept the things you cannot change? Write, draw, dance, or sculpt your request.

Imagine being nurtured by the inspiration, love, and support of your womb-circle. Imagine being rocked, supported, and enfolded by them. They caress your wounds. They hold your dreams tenderly. They gather your tears. Receive the gifts of the nurturing womb.

Reach out to the women in your life this week. Share with them your need for a tender, nurturing presence. Allow them to be the feminine face of god to you.

The Gifts of the Pushy Womb

Do you desire the gifts of the pushy womb: An acknowledgment of your power; the courage to change the things you can? Out of what situations or into what new adventures do you need the courage to move? Write, draw, dance, or sculpt your request.

Imagine the womb-circle quickening in its breath, contracting, readying to push you forth: Out of an abusive relationship or a depleting situation. Into a new career or relationship adventure. Imagine the inspiration, love, and support of your circle, encouraging you to exert, initiate, and move on your own behalf, thrusting you forward into your own life. Receive the gifts of the pushy womb.

Reach out to the women in your life this week. Share with them your need for courage, challenge, and support. Allow them to be the feminine face of god to you.

Breathing in . . . I value the women in my life.
  Breathing out . . . They are the feminine face of god to me.
Breathing in . . . They remind me of the truth about myself
  Breathing out . . . When I forget.

Acts of Courage

As the Mother of All Living, Eve picked the good fruit of life. It was good and satisfied hunger. It was pleasant to the eye and offered pleasure. It was wise and opened the way to self-discovery and understanding. She invites those among us who are curious, who lust for life in all its fluidity, to dare with her by biting into life and the fullness of its possibility. She speaks from the depths of us, "Bite into your life and the fullness of its possibility."

1. Recall a time when your mother reached for the apple, a moment when she remembered her former glory and bit into her life and the fullness of its possibility.

   Individual Response: *My mother bit into the apple when she _____.*

   Examples: My mother bit into the apple and went to law school at age fifty-eight.

   My mother bit into the apple by going away alone one weekend a month for a personal retreat.

   Communal Response: *Mother, we celebrate your act of courage.*

2. Recall a time when you reached for the apple, a moment when you remembered your former glory and bit into your life and the fullness of its possibility.

   Individual Response: *I bit into the apple of my life when I _____.*

   Examples: I bit into the apple and acknowledged my love for a woman.

   I bit into the apple by working only three days a week and painting the other four.

   Communal Response: *Sister, we celebrate your act of courage.*

3. Pass Eve's apple around the circle. Before biting into it, receive the support of the circle of women.

Individual Response: *I will bite into the apple of my* _____.

Examples: I will bite into the apple of my creativity and write a book.

I will bite into the apple of my sexuality and celebrate my body's responses.

Communal Response: *Sister, we support you to act with courage.*

Breathing in . . . I value the women in my life.
  Breathing out . . . They are the feminine face of god to me.
Breathing in . . . They remind me of the truth about myself
  Breathing out . . . When I forget.

19

Imagine a woman who has relinquished the desire for intellectual safety and approval.

A woman who makes a powerful statement with every word she speaks, every action she takes.

Who asserts to herself the right to reorder the world.

Outrageous Words
and Forbidden Acts

Some of us missed the second wave of feminism in the late '60s and early '70s. We were immersed in fundamentalist traditions that kept us isolated from the political movements in the wider culture. We were dealing with the aftermath of growing up in severely dysfunctional homes—the kind of home situations no one wanted to hear about because they were so "depressing." We were struggling with our addictions to food, drugs, alcohol, and relationships. Addictions that kept us comatose, numbed out until we were ready to walk through our personal pasts. Or we were immersed in the isolation of being Mrs. Somebody, as fearful of those angry feminist "bra-burners" as our husbands were.

Our "consciousness raising" came much later than our feminist sisters. The "knight in shining armor" mythology shattered as we found ourselves divorced and the sole financial and emotional provider for our children. We sought support at a local women's center and began to listen to women's stories, shedding the competitive attitudes of a lifetime. We stumbled into a self-help meeting and a woman said "Goddess" instead of the compulsory "God" in the twelve steps, and we wondered how she got the courage to commit such a heretical act. Our therapist suggested we read *The Second Sex* or *The Creation of Patriarchy,* and we were stunned that women were writing such powerful treatises and that we knew nothing about them. We showed up at seminary to major in religious education, the appropriate focus for young women, only to discover most of our classmates were "radical" women going into the ordained ministry. We relocated and found ourselves drawn to the local Unitarian church. We sat with tears in our eyes every Sunday listening to the preacher. *Her* words resonated with our deepest experience in a way that the words of male ministers had never been able to do.

It is always in the company of women that we are reminded of our common heritage as women. A heritage that reaches beyond "the beginning" defined by men to the "very beginning" when the divine was imagined as woman. We discover that we are surrounded by a courageous cloud of witnesses—their experience and stories, their ideas and images, their creativity and outrage become healing resources for us. No longer asking the question, "What's wrong with me?" we are freed from our obsession with the works, words, and lives of men. Self-possessed, we step outside of patriarchal thought and immerse ourselves in women's history, philosophy, theology, creativity, and spirituality. Receive Gerda Lerner's strong challenge:

> To step outside of patriarchal thought means: . . . Being skeptical toward every known system of thought; being critical of all assumptions, ordering values and definitions. . . . Being critical toward our own thought, which is, after all, thought trained in the patriarchal tradition. Finally, it means developing intellectual courage, the

courage to stand alone, the courage to reach farther than our grasp, the courage to risk failure.

Perhaps the greatest challenge to thinking women is the challenge to move from the desire for safety and approval to the most "unfeminine" quality of all—that of intellectual arrogance, the supreme hubris which asserts to itself the right to reorder the world. The hubris of the godmakers, the hubris of the male system builders.

Women have been warned against exhibiting hubris ("arrogant pride") all of their lives. Our feminist sisters support us to be arrogantly full of ourselves for the salvation of a planet out of balance and in danger of annihilating itself. In their every word, we hear the affirmation, *"It is right and good that you are woman. Be full of yourself!"*

Daughter of woman, relinquish your desire for intellectual safety and approval.
Makes a powerful statement with every word you speak, every action you take.
Assert to yourself the right to reorder the world.

Extending the Circle

Begin a four-month immersion in the works of women with your daughter, coworker, friend, or women's circle. Surround yourselves with women's ideas, history, stories, books, films, art, music, and spirituality. Reflect on how you feel about your life, body, relationships, dreams, and goals while engaging these woman-affirming resources.

Judy Chicago's art project *The Dinner Party* celebrates the contributions and achievements of 1,038 women. The project is described and illustrated in an inspiring book you will find in your local library or women's center. Throughout the four months, read ten entries at the start of each a day to become acquainted with your heritage. Inspired by your woman-heritage, become a system-builder, a god-maker. Reorder your family and relationships, your workplace, community, and world from a woman's perspective.

MONTH 1: *Women's History*

Gather more of the fragments of women's stories from the margins of history and religion. These books will inspire your quest for a heritage, a history, a noble lineage, reaching back to the *very* beginning: *The Creation of Patriarchy* and *The Creation of Feminist Consciousness,* Gerda Lerner; *When God Was a Woman,* Merlin Stone; *The Once and Future Goddess,* Elinor Gadon.

MONTH 2: *Women's Ways of Knowing*

Women experience the world differently than do men. Reclaim your unique woman-intelligence and bring its gifts into the world. Allow the works of these creative thinkers to inspire you: *Vindication of the Rights of Women,* Mary Wollstonecraft; *The Second Sex,* Simone de Beauvoir; *Women's Reality,* Anne Wilson Schaef; *Of Woman Born,*

Adrienne Rich; *Sister Outsider,* Audre Lorde; *Blood, Bread, and Roses: How Menstruation Created The World,* Judy Grahn.

MONTH 3: *Women Writers and Poets*

Allow the brilliance of women's words to inspire your own writing. Be full of yourself! Write a novel, compose a poem: *A Room of One's Own,* Virginia Woolf; *Made from This Earth,* Susan Griffin; *Circling the Waters,* Marge Piercy; *A Daughter's Geography,* Ntozake Shange; *Getting Home Alive,* Aurora and Rosario Morales; *Cries of the Spirit,* Marilyn Sewell; *The Temple of My Familiar,* Alice Walker.

MONTH 4: *Women Artists, Dancers, and Musicians*

Surround yourself with women's music, images, and movements this month. In response, allow the creative fruits of your womb to thrust forth: *The Birth Project,* Judy Chicago; "Shadows on the Dime," Ferron; "A Circle Is Cast," Libana; "City Down," Castleberry & Dupree; *The Spirit Moves,* Carla De Sola.

Breathing in . . . I am surrounded
Breathing out . . . By a courageous community of women.
Breathing in . . . Their experience and stories,
Breathing out . . . Their ideas and images,
Breathing in . . . Their creativity and outrage,
Breathing out . . . Are healing resources for me.
Breathing in . . . They remind me of the truth about myself
Breathing out . . . When I forget.

Sisters, We Remember You

Courageous women have challenged the prevailing views about women from within the Judeo-Christian community for over a thousand years by assuming equality with the male translators, interpreters, and commentators of the Bible. Read through the following "Litany of Remembrance," acknowledging these women. Allow their courage to support you to assert your right to reorder the religious/spiritual community of which you are a part. The litany was inspired by chapter 7 in Gerda Lerner's *Creation of Feminist Consciousness.*

At your next women's gathering or church forum, acknowledge the courage of these women by naming them aloud in your circle. After the entire "Litany of Remembrance" has been read, conclude by saying, "Sisters, we remember you. We celebrate your forbidden acts."

- ⇝ Unnamed Montanist women (second century C.E.)—Assumed prophetic roles in the church, claiming Eve as their champion.

- ⇝ Hildegard of Bingen (1098–1179)—Brilliant mystic, abbess, preacher, teacher, counselor, and prolific writer.

- ⇝ Christine de Pizan (1365–c. 1430)—Single mother, biographer, illustrator, biblical commentator; defender of women.

- ⇝ Isotta Nogarola (1418–1466)—Learned Renaissance woman and biblical commentator; defender of Eve.

- ⇝ Laura Cereta (1469–1499)—Woman humanist and mathematician; defender of Eve.

- Marguerite d' Angouleme (1492–1549)—Queen of Navarre and humanist author, feminist theologian.

- Anne Askew (sixteenth century)—Defender of a woman's right to interpret scripture; burned as a heretic in 1546.

- Jane Anger (sixteenth century)—Biblical commentator and pamphleteer; defender of Eve's superiority.

- Rachel Speght (seventeenth century)—Brilliant deconstructionist of misogynistic views; defender of Eve's equality.

- Ester Sowernam (seventeenth century)—Aggressive deconstructionist; defender of Eve as "the mother of all living."

- Sarah Fyge (1669–1722)—Banished from her father's house for writing a poem that celebrated Eve's goodness.

- Antoinette Bourignon (1606–1680)—Pietist preacher and religious writer; defender of the androgynous image of god.

- Margaret Fell (1614–1702)—Quaker teacher, preacher, writer; defended women's active role in ministry; imprisoned for her beliefs.

- Mary Astell (1666–1731)—Biblical commentator; challenged the authority of patriarchal interpreters of scripture.

- Ann Lee (1736–1784)—Shaker preacher and teacher; defender of Sophia, the female aspect of the androgynous divine.

- Joanna Southcott (1750–1814)—Prophet; defender of women who are called to bring the knowledge of the good fruit to humankind.

- Julia Smith (1792–1878)—Feminist and abolitionist; translator of the Bible from its original languages: Greek, Hebrew, and Latin.

- Sarah Moore Grimke (1792–1873)—Feminist and abolitionist, biblical commentator; defender of Eve's equality, freedom, and intellect.

Sisters, we remember you. We celebrate your forbidden acts.

Breathing in . . . I relinquish my desire
  Breathing out . . . for intellectual safety and approval.
Breathing in . . . I make a powerful statement with every word I speak
  Breathing out . . . Every action I take.
Breathing in . . . I assert to myself
  Breathing out . . . the right to reorder the world.

20

Imagine a woman who has grown in knowledge and love of herself.

A woman who has vowed faithfulness to her own life and capacities.

Who remains loyal to herself. Regardless.

Growing in Knowledge
and Love of Myself

My life as I had known it fell apart at Princeton Seminary. Fundamentalism had been the organizing focus of my time and energy, and God the father and the Bible had shaped my every thought, feeling, and action since childhood. Having assumed theological equality while at Princeton, I was slowly dismantling the throne of God and the infallibility of the scripture. I was being drawn inward to reestablish a relationship to myself and my own inner wisdom, yet I had forgotten the way home. I needed an escort.

Jean Hauser, skillful therapist and guide, was my first escort into the rich resources of my inner life. I arrived at her office ready to talk about my past. There was a certain safety in my attempts to understand the complexities of childhood with words. She patiently listened to my stories and then asked if I was willing to try a relaxation exercise. In the silence, she gently invited me to turn inward and descend into my inner life. At times I couldn't handle the discomfort of the silence, so I retreated into the safety of words again. Over time, I became fascinated with what was emerging from the deep places within me. I'd walk into Jean's office and announce, "No talking today. Take me down!"

Jean did not seek to influence my experience. She used a simple relaxation technique to support my descent. Then she left me alone while I traveled through a magical forest, discovering paths and clearings, encountering snakes and trees, and befriending the richness of my own inner life. Jean sat in the silence as a compassionate witness to the tears and laughter, screams and moans, movements and stillness that accompanied my transformative journey. Each session became a sacred drama performed deep within the forest of my being. Sometimes it seemed important to tell her about my adventures. Most of the time it was enough that I had experienced them. During our two years together, I learned to trust my inner life, to discern its intricate design, and to listen to its healing truth. I discovered that the deepest impulse of my being was to heal into the present. As I descended into my own life, I reconnected to this impulse and tapped a reservoir of transformative resources.

I believe a woman discovers the way home to herself in a quiet descent into the richness of her own life, not in the rat race for equal pay and position, in the adoption of a traditional or feminist persona, or in the ability to articulate the intricacies of her childhood. In the descent, she reverses the tendency to look outside herself for salvation. In the "deep places" she reunites with her essential self and reclaims her natural capacities. Based on this conviction, I include the "Home Is Always Waiting" meditation in each workshop, retreat, support group, or private session I facilitate. You have experienced excerpts of it throughout the book. Here I have included the entire meditation. May it be a reminder of your own inner resources when you forget yourself. May it escort you home when you wander away from yourself. May it bring a smile to your soul every day of your life. May it support you to remain loyal to yourself. Regardless.

Home Is Always Waiting

A Beginning

In the very beginning of life, you were acquainted with the exquisite natural resources of your breath, your woman-body, and your spiritual center. You breathed deeply into your belly. You loved your body. You were in touch with the spirit resident within your life.

Over time, the girl-child becomes disconnected from the home within her. Caught in the swirls of others, twisted into the shapes of others, depleted by the demands of others, her breath becomes shallow. She ignores her body. She looks outside herself for salvation and validation, forgetting the rich resources within.

In the fullness of time, we become dizzy from swirling, our lives ache from being twisted out of shape, our beings become depleted as a result of servicing others with our attention and energy. Weary, we long to return home, yet we have forgotten the way.

Rediscover the way home. Home is always waiting. It is as near as a conscious breath, conscious contact with your woman-body, and a descent into your spiritual center. You have everything you need within the rich resources of your own life.

A Conscious Breath

Let us begin by making conscious contact with the breath. Turn your attention inward. Become conscious of the breath and its faithful rhythm, supporting you the length of your days.

If you are particularly distracted, you may find it helpful to count each inhalation and exhalation. The breath will escort you into this moment. Pay attention to the coming and going of the breath for at least ten inhalations and exhalations. Breathe into this moment with each inhalation. Release anything that is not of this moment with each exhalation.

Allow sighs, sounds, and yawns to ride on the back of your breath, releasing the accumulation of your day, of a lifetime. Life becomes simpler, clearer, and lighter as you come into this moment, paying attention to your breath and letting go of all distraction. Weave an affirmation into each breath: *"I am enough. Just as I am. I am enough. Without doing anything."*

Notice the depth of your breath.

- ⊷ Place your hands on your upper chest. Inhale, expanding your chest with the breath. Exhale, slowly letting go of all burdens that are not yours to carry. Continue to breathe into your upper chest for two more breaths.

- ⊷ Now place your hands on the sides of your rib cage. Inhale deeply, pushing the breath against your ribs. Exhale. Continue to fill your rib cavity for two more breaths, deepening your capacity to hold the nourishing breath of life.

- ⊷ Place your hands on your abdomen. Inhale deeply, imagining the breath as a great wave filling your belly. Allow your belly to swell. This is a deep breath. Exhale as the wave retreats, leaving nourishment and fulfillment in its wake. Continue to breathe deeply into your belly for two breaths.

- ⊷ Now place your hands on your lower back. Breathe into your lower back, the location of your kidneys, the well of life-giving energy within you. Breathe deeply into the well within you. Allow this deep breath to nourish you, to enrich you, to fill you. Continue to breathe deeply into your lower back for two more breaths.

- ⊷ Bring your arms to your sides and continue to breathe deeply. Inhale, as the full swell moves upward from your abdomen, into your rib cavity, and then into the upper chest. Exhale, as the wave retreats downward from your chest, your rib cavity, and your abdomen, leaving in its wake serenity. Continue this deep breathing for two more breaths.

Breathe into this moment. Imagine this moment as a clearing in the forest of your busy life. Imagine the breath escorting you into the clearing, into the moment. With each inhalation, gather all of yourself from the far reaches of your life. Gather your feelings, your thoughts, your attention and energy home again into this moment.

With each exhalation, let go of all distraction.

Breathing in . . . I acknowledge this moment.
    Breathing out . . . I let go of the past, an hour ago, a day ago, a year ago,
    a decade ago.
Breathing in . . . I enter into this moment.
    Breathing out . . . I let go of the future, a day from now, a year from
    now, a decade from now.

Breathing in . . . I receive the fullness of this moment.
    Breathing out . . . I have everything I need to be here, now.

If your attention moves away from home, away from your breath, away from this moment, notice the distraction without judgment, and then practice returning home. There will always be distractions. Our life-practice is to return. Home is always waiting. It is as near as a conscious breath.

Make Conscious Contact with Your Woman-Body

Imagine that you are in an ancient forest. You have roots like the trees surrounding you. You are as grounded, as connected to Mother Earth as a tree. You are held, supported, and nourished by Her. Acknowledge the firm ground that holds you.

Everything breathes in the forest. Breathe deeply and savor the breath of life that flows in and through and around you. As you inhale, imagine the breath rising up from the rich earth beneath you. As you exhale, imagine releasing the breath into the cool and moist air around you. Weave an affirmation into each breath: *"My body is enough. Just as it is. My body is good. There is no blemish."*

Make conscious contact with your woman-body by taking a gentle walk over and around it—using tender self-touch or massage, gentle movement or stretch, or the quietness of your imagination, inviting your breath to reach toward each part of your body.

At your own pace, create a Meditation of Acknowledgment. Beginning at the top of your head or the bottom of your feet, slowly move, touch, or imagine each part of your body, personalizing the affirmation: *"My nose is good just as it is. There is no blemish." "My breasts are good just as they are. There is no blemish."*
Bless your woman-body in the silence.

To complete your Meditation of Acknowledgment, turn a merciful eye toward your body. Look upon it with loving-kindness as you pay special attention to the areas it has been difficult to acknowledge—a scar, a place trespassed by another, a layer of protective fat, an untouchable part. Are you ashamed of certain parts of your body? Proud of others? Notice what is true for you without judgment. Meet each response and feeling with the breath. Acknowledge your response on the inhalation, then let go of it on the exhalation. Affirm: *"My woman-body is holy. Just as it is. There is no blemish."*

If your attention moves away from home, away from your body and breath, caught in familiar swirls of regret, worry, longing, obsessive thought or concern, notice the distraction without judgment and practice returning home. Breathe again into this moment, letting go of the past and the future. There will always be distractions. Our life-practice is to return. Home is always waiting. It is as near as a conscious breath and conscious contact with your woman-body.

A Descent into the Rich Resources of Your Inner Life

Imagine yourself as a leaf let go of by an autumn tree . . .
a leaf slowly and gradually descending toward the ground . . .
its descent cushioned by the breath of life . . .
a leaf touching the ground in the forest deep within your being.
You rise from the ground, thanking the leaf for transporting you so
    gently.

Everything is breathing in the forest. Savor the breath of life flowing in and around you. Inhale deeply as the breath rises from the rich earth beneath you. Release the breath into the cool and moist air around you. Weave an affirmation into each breath:

Breathing in . . . I come home to rich resources of my inner life.
    Breathing out . . . Home is always waiting.

Your attention moves upward and you notice the trees reaching arm in arm for the sky. You become a tree. Your feet grow roots extending deep into the ground. Your arms become branches stretching high into the sky. You sway with the breeze. The birds of the forest dance with you as they leap from branch to branch. You see many things from your new height.

Breathing in . . . I am rooted and grounded in the earth.
    Breathing out . . . I come home to the ground of my being.
Breathing in . . . I am expansive and fill the universe.
    Breathing out . . . I come home to the spaciousness of my being.

A nearby stream calls to you, "Come and play." In a moment, you are at the stream, splashing in its bouncing waters. As you are drying off in the warm sunlight pouring through the forest canopy, a path opens up before you and invites you to follow it to a special place. You accept the invitation and follow the path.

Breathing in . . . I am escorted on the path of life.
    Breathing out . . . I come home to my inner guidance.

The path leads you deep within the forest to the edge of a clearing . . . a magical open space surrounded by a ring of ancient redwoods, forming an outer circle, and by a sparkling stream, forming an inner circle. As you peek through the stately redwood circle, you recognize the clearing as the home you once knew in the very beginning of your life. You cross the stream. You enter the clearing. You are home.

Breathing in . . . I return home.
    Breathing out . . . Home is always waiting.

For the final moments of this meditation, in the quietness of your healing imagination or in your journal-sketchpad, reflect on the images that surface while you linger in the clearing. Draw them. Dance them. Write them. Breathe into them. Come home to the rich resources of your inner life.

Daughter of Woman, Home is always waiting. It is as near as a conscious breath, conscious contact with your woman-body, and a descent into the rich resources of your inner life.

Daughter of Woman,
As a sign of your love and respect for yourself,
Remain loyal to yourself
In tender times and turbulent times.
In graceful moments and in awkward situations.
In flowing times and in seasons of stagnation.
In fullness and in emptiness.
In fear and in courage.
In trouble and in beauty.
With all that you are and all you shall become.
For the rest of your life.

Daughter of Woman,
Love yourself.
Regardless.

About the Author

Patricia Lynn Reilly holds a Master of Divinity degree from Princeton Theological Seminary and a postgraduate certification in Women's Spirituality and Feminist Theology from the Women's Theological Center. As the founder of Open Window Creations, she conducts women's spirituality, creativity, and self-esteem workshops and publishes inspirational books and resources. Patricia is the author of:

A God Who Looks Like Me: Discovering a Woman-Affirming
    Spirituality (Ballantine, 1995)
Be Full of Yourself!: The Journey from Self-Criticism to Self-Celebration
    (Open Window Creations, 1998)
A Vow of Faithfulness (to be published by Conari Press in Spring 2000)

Companion Resources

Patricia Lynn Reilly offers a variety of workshops, retreats, and presentations based on the content of this book. She has also developed woman-affirming resources to enhance the reader's experience of the book, including:

"Imagine a Woman" postcard (eight stanzas of the poem)
"Imagine a Woman" greeting card (twenty stanzas of the poem)
"Home Is Always Waiting Meditation" audiocassette

If you would like a schedule of upcoming events and a brochure of companion resources, write, call, or e-mail:

Open Window Creations
P. O. Box 8615
Berkeley, California 94707
510-530-4859
E-Mail: patricia@openwindowcreations.com
Web site: www.openwindowcreations.com

CONARI PRESS, established in 1987, publishes books on topics ranging from psychology, spirituality, and women's history to sexuality, parenting, and personal growth. Our main goal is to publish quality books that will make a difference in people's lives—both how we feel about ourselves and how we relate to one another.

Our readers are our most important resource, and we value your input, suggestions, and ideas. We'd love to hear from you—after all, we are publishing books for you!

To request our latest book catalog, or to be added to our mailing list, please contact:

CONARI PRESS
2550 Ninth Street, Suite 101
Berkeley, California 94710-2551
800-685-9595   510-649-7175
fax: 510-649-7190   e-mail: conari@conari.com
www.conari.com